To y
May your life
be full of
Miracles!

Love,
Kathy

IT IS DONE!

by

Kathy Lewis

This book was written by Kathy Lewis
2000 Powers Ferry Center, Suite 2-3
Marietta, Georgia   30067
770-956-8252 / 800-229-8556
Fax 770-952-3289 / email: kathyl@capinst.com

© Copyright 2002, Kathy Lewis

Notice of Rights:

All rights reserved. No part of this book may be reproduced or transmitted in any form by means, electronic, mechanical, photo-copying, recording or otherwise, without the prior written permission of the author. For information on getting permission for reprints and excerpts, contact Kathy Lewis.

Notice of Liability:

Every effort has been made to ensure the accuracy of this book. While every precaution has been taken in the preparation of this book, the author shall not have any liability to any person or entity with respect to any loss or damage caused or alleged to be caused directly or indirectly by the information contained in this book.

ISBN 1-59405-051-1   Published by N2Print

Printed and bound in the United States of America.

DEDICATION

To Jack and Joyce Lewis, my first spiritual teachers, who gave me life and nurtured the belief that I have within me everything I need to make it good.

IT
IS
DONE!

TABLE OF CONTENTS

Foreword xi
Miracles Still Happen! 1
The Miracle of My First Home 13
The Miracle of the Bookcase 19
The Miracle of the Job Interview 21
The Miracle of Turning Failure into Triumph 29
The Miracle on the Expressway ....….........38
The Miracle of My New Career 45
The Miracle of My Free Truck 54
The Miracle of Collecting on a Debt 59
The Miracle of the Lost Ring 61
I Start My New Career 65
The Miracle of My Third New Career 73
The Miracle of My Fourth New Career ….................79
The Miracle of the Red Dress ....…......................84
The Miracle of My Own School 87
Another Miracle of *"Sleeping On A Problem
   and Waking Up With An Answer"* 89
The Miracle of the Classroom Space 93
It Was Time to Make Some Changes 95
The Miracle of My Classroom Desks
   and Chairs ……..101
The Miracle of the Lost Emerald ......…...............103
Illness Strikes — Followed by a
   Miraculous Healing ..…......................................105
It Was Time for Some Professional Help .....….......110
Another Miracle Answered by
   "Sleeping on It"...121
The Miracle of the Free Fax Machine ......…..........124
The Joy of *"Positive Affirmations"* 126

The Miracle of My New Car ....…............................131
The Miracle of My *"Getaway Weekend"*.....................134
Miracles at the Airport ....…….......136
Tragedy Strikes ....…….....................................141
The Miracle of My New Home ....…….........148
The Miracle of My New Office ....…….....155
My World Falls Apart ....…….........................159
God Gives Me a Sign That Things Will
    Get Better ……...............…….................... 165
The Miracle of My School's New Direction ….....…..168
I Meet the Man of My Dreams ....……........173
My School Expands in Yet Another
    Direction ....……...............................178
The Miracle of the Prayer of Gratitude —
    Getting My Employees Involved ….........................181
The Miracle of Getting College
    Accreditation 185
Affirming a *"Computer Geek"* to Help
    With a Technical Issue 186
I Have a Past Life Regression ....…….....................189
The Miracles Continue ....…….................... 194

FOREWORD

My friends and associates have been telling me for years that I should write a book about all of the incredible miracles that have occurred in my life, and there have been many!

I have come to accept these miracles as the most natural thing in the world and am surprised when people show amazement or disbelief when I relate these stories.

After all, God has always said, *"I will give you the desires of your heart,"* so your prayer should be a prayer of gratitude accepting that your request has ***ALREADY BEEN ANSWERED — IT IS ALREADY DONE!***

I always end my prayers by saying, *"Thank You, Lord! **IT IS DONE!**"* because I have total faith God has already responded — as He will for you ***IF YOU WILL ONLY BELIEVE!***

In my book I mention a wonderful spiritual counselor named Jack Bernard Moon. Jack now lives in Florida and may be reached by email at:

www.jackbmoon.com

I would love to hear your comments after reading this book. I'm sure many of you have also experienced miracles in your life and I welcome the opportunity to share these experiences with you!

You may email me at: **kathyl@capinst.com**

MAY YOUR LIFE BE FULL OF MIRACLES!

MIRACLES STILL HAPPEN!

I found it when I was sorting through my jewelry box. It was a mustard seed pendant that my mother wore on her watchband back when I was a little girl. My gosh, this thing was almost 50 years old! I had forgotten all about it!

I remembered the significance of having faith the size of a mustard seed and decided to pull out my Bible and look it up. It was in Matthew, verse 17:20: *"If ye have faith as a grain of mustard seed, ye shall say unto this mountain, 'Remove hence to yonder place;' and it shall remove; and nothing shall be impossible unto you."*

These are pretty powerful words! Having faith no greater than the mustard seed, the tiniest seed in the world, means *"nothing shall be impossible to you,"*–**"NOTHING SHALL BE IMPOSSIBLE TO YOU."** True miracles could occur.

I started thinking about miracles and realized that my life was full of miracles, almost on a daily basis!

What about my Mother? She wore this mustard seed pendant on her watchband; did she believe in miracles?

My Mother did relate one incident that happened when we kids were very small. My Dad, a linotype operator, had been laid off from his job and, with a wife and four little children to support, I imagine he was pretty anxious to find another job. When he heard about a possible job opening in the next town, he called and made an appointment to interview, left some money with my mother to take care of us, and was on his way.

He was gone longer than anticipated and my Mother told me that her funds got very low. Down to her last *two dollars*, she had no idea how to feed all of us until my Dad returned. She stood at the bureau in her bedroom, holding those two dollar bills in her hand, frantically running through her mind how she would make it work.

Finally, she let out a sigh, opened the bureau drawer, and dropped the two dollar bills into the drawer. As she pushed the drawer shut, the mustard seed pendant hanging on her watchband got caught in the drawer and she had to pull it open to extricate the pendant.

Suddenly she stopped and stared at that pendant, remembering the significance of the mustard seed. It occurred to her that perhaps she should send a prayer to God, asking for help.

She prayed, *"Lord, I don't know what to do. I don't know how I'm going to feed all of us with these two dollars, so I'm asking for Your help. Please help me, Lord."* She shut the drawer and went about her business.

Later in the day our next-door neighbor stopped by to see if she could pick up anything for my Mother at the grocery store. My Mother said, *"Sure, just wait one minute while I get some money."* All the time she was headed to the bedroom she was frantically trying to decide what she could buy with her paltry two dollars.

It Is Done!

She pulled open the drawer — *AND STARED AT A TEN DOLLAR BILL LYING WHERE THE TWO DOLLARS HAD BEEN BEFORE!*

She was stunned! *"I'm not crazy,"* she said to herself. *"I know there were only two dollars in that drawer!"* And then she stopped, remembering her prayer to God...well it appeared that her prayer had been answered! She told me that ten dollars was enough to take care of us until my Dad returned. This was a true miracle!

My Mother related this story to me in a hushed tone while she kept looking over her shoulder, perhaps thinking she would be struck by lightning for revealing her secret; who knows?

I think my Mother believed that one should never call upon God for help unless it was a dire emergency and all other avenues had been exhausted. One certainly didn't ask God for trivial things, since God was much too busy dealing with the crises of the world.

The issue of *"praying for what we wanted"* wasn't discussed, although I know both of my parents believed in God. I do remember being told by my parents that I could call on God when I was in trouble and He would help me, and, as far back as I can remember, I honestly and truly believed this. I always had the strange notion that I *"had special protection"* and to this day I still tell everyone *"I have special protection."*

Why did I believe I had *"special protection*?" I have no idea. However, as I look back over my life I recall numerous occasions when this was all too true.

I remember one occasion when I was in kindergarten that I waited and waited in the parking lot after school for my Dad to come and take me home. On this day, he was very late, which was most unusual for my Dad.

Then a car pulled up beside me and a big man rolled down the window. He told me my Dad couldn't come for me, but he had asked this man to take me home. He then urged me to get into the car with him. I remember a *"feeling"* (which I now attribute to my guardian angel) that I shouldn't get in that car and I told the man I couldn't.

Despite all of his coaxing, I wouldn't budge! Finally, he got out of the car and came toward me, I'm sure to forcibly put me in that car!

To this day I don't know what happened, except that the man stopped, looked at me strangely, then turned around very quickly, got in his car and tore out of the parking lot! Very strange! As he was pulling away, my Dad came into view. He apologized for being late, blaming it on a flat tire. I attempted to tell my Dad about the man who tried to pick me up, but since I was prone to making up stories at that time in my life, and since there was no sign of this man, I know my Dad didn't believe me.

I have no doubt in my mind that this man was up to no good, and I also have absolutely no doubt that **SOMETHING** stopped him dead in his tracks. My guardian angel, perhaps? The great thing about guardian angels is that they are always there for us even if we aren't consciously aware of them! ***Thank you, guardian angel!***

It Is Done!

I remember another incident that occurred when I was 17 years old. I worked a part-time job in a department store downtown each afternoon when I got out of school and each Saturday. The bus didn't run by my house on Saturday so I had to walk about a mile or more to the nearest bus stop to catch the bus.

One Saturday morning as I walked along the sidewalk toward the bus stop I noticed a man on the opposite side of the street. I found it very strange that this man was dressed in a heavy trench coat, since it was in the middle of summer, but I soon found out why he was wearing that trench coat! When this man spotted me, he began running across the street toward me, yelling at me!

As if that wasn't enough to frighten the living daylights out of me, he came to a halt in front of me, all the time yelling obscenities, then jerked open his coat — to reveal a totally naked body with a full-blown erection!

I was stunned! Remember, I was just an innocent 17-year-old kid who had never seen a naked man in my life! So what did I do? I started laughing! I looked at this man and said, *"Now don't you feel silly! What do you think you're doing?"*

I don't think this was the reaction he expected. He gazed at me with a stupid look on his face and looked down in horror as his full erection suddenly went limp, at which point he took off running! I laughed my head off! I thought it was the funniest thing I had ever seen.

I told everybody at work what happened and told my parents when I got home and was really bewildered by their reaction. They got very upset and immediately called the police, and my Dad informed me that from that point forward he would be taking me to the bus stop on Saturday mornings.

The police informed us that this man, who was eventually caught, had attacked and raped two women right there in our neighborhood and they considered me *"one lucky little lady."*

As for me, I don't think it was luck! I think, once again, my guardian angel guided me to laugh rather than scream in terror, which is exactly where that man got his power. Laughing at him was the last thing he expected, and it flustered him so much that he took off! **Thank you, guardian angel!**

I could go on and on about incidents like these that kept me out of harm's way, but I must admit that one particular incident made me a *"true believer!"*

When I was in my mid-twenties, a very handsome young man began attending my church and had all the girls swooning. I was really surprised when he started spending time with me, since I sure didn't consider myself the type of girl to attract the *"hunks"* of the world and I was thrilled when he asked me out.

The other girls in my church group were quite envious and grumbled among themselves that they couldn't understand why he chose ME! We scheduled a time to get together — and something came up and I had to cancel. We re-scheduled — and something came up and he had to cancel. We re-scheduled again — and something came up and I had to cancel.

This was getting comical! When we re-scheduled for the fourth time and once again one of us had to cancel, I figured there was a reason this wasn't working out, and I suggested perhaps we should forego getting together.

We drifted apart after that and eventually he stopped attending my church. I forgot all about him until one night a few months later I was watching the local news. I was stunned to see a picture of this man on the TV screen as the newscaster recounted a horrifying story!

This **SAME MAN** was picked up by the police after he brutally murdered a girl in a local apartment complex! He stabbed her so hard that the knife went through the floor into the ceiling of the apartment below! Neighbors heard her screams and called the police. When they arrived, they followed the trail of blood outside the apartment building and found him sitting on the steps, holding his hand. Apparently he had cut off two of his own fingers during the attack!

It turned out that this man had been released from a mental hospital in Florida! He told the police that *"God told him to kill that girl!"* Whew! Another close call! I then understood that, once again, my *"special protection"* had kept me out of harm's way. That incident really shook me up and I realized that meeting men at church was no guarantee that I would be safe! Believe me, I was much more careful about who I accepted a date from after that experience!

After this incident it seemed that I was at the church every time the doors opened since I felt I needed to *"repay"* God for once again keeping me out of harm's way. I joined a couple of church committees; I attended a Bible study group, and went to a children's home each week as a volunteer. In other words, I was running myself ragged, trying to do everything I could to make myself **"acceptable and worthy of God's love."**

It finally caught up with me one night when I returned from my weekly visit to the children's home. I was exhausted, dejected, and disappointed in myself. I walked into my bedroom, sat down at the foot of the bed, and started crying. I couldn't do this anymore.

I started talking to God, *"Lord, I can't do this anymore. I hate being on these committees; I'm bored to tears in the Bible study, and I'm just not a 'kid' person; I dread going to the children's home each week. I can't continue this way. I know I'm a disappointment to You, Lord, but I'm miserable and tired and frustrated. Please forgive me, Lord. I just can't be what You want me to be!"*

The entire time I was speaking to God, I was banging my fist on my bed, with tears running down my face. I finally calmed down and sat there sniffling. Then, something very unusual happened. **God spoke to me!** I heard Him very clearly. He said, *"Kathy, who asked you to?"*

I was stunned! God speaking to me? Was it really God? I ventured a question, *"God, is that You? What do you mean? Isn't this what I'm supposed to do?"* I waited.

I heard Him again. He said, *"Kathy, you take time to get to know **ME**! I'll make it known to you where you're needed."*

What did that mean — *"Get to know HIM?"* Wasn't that why I spent so much time at church? Wasn't that the only way to get to know Him? No answer was forthcoming. I was so overwhelmed that I couldn't sleep. I kept running it over and over in my mind. **God spoke to ME! To ME!** I knew my life would never be the same.

I went about my daily routine, going to work, going to church — but nothing was the same. I kept thinking about God's message to *"Get to know **ME**."* How would I do that? It was difficult for me to sit in church and listen to the sermon about **"GOD UP THERE AND SINFUL ME DOWN HERE."**

It didn't make sense. The church seemed to be advocating the premise that *"God was a distant, vengeful, jealous God Who wished to remain separate from us."* If that were true, then why did God say, *"Get to know **ME**?"*

That was the beginning. The barrier was down. When I began talking to God as a friend the same way I talked to all of my other friends, that was when the miracles began.

It was all so simple. I could talk to God, tell Him what I wanted, believe I could have it, and wait for it to happen. I stopped questioning whether or not I was ***worthy*** to receive God's blessings. There is no ***worthiness*** factor; there is only a ***request*** factor. *"Ask and ye shall receive..."* *"You have not because you ask not..."*

While I wasn't attending church as regularly as I had in the past, I was still reading everything I could get my hands on and talking to everyone I knew about my experience, trying to find out if any of them had experienced anything similar. The people at church looked at me as if I was crazy so I stopped talking about it, but it never left my mind.

I started having some really strange dreams. Even though it's been about 25 years, I still remember one particularly vivid dream as if it happened yesterday.

In my dream I heard a knock at my apartment door and when I opened the door I stood facing a group of *"beings,"* all dressed in black hooded robes. Where their face should have been I saw only two very large **RED EYES!** I was terrified!

These *"beings"* never spoke a word...they just started slowly moving toward me. I screamed in terror and began backing up. The farther I backed up, the closer they moved toward me. I had the sense that they were trying to back me into my bedroom, which was dark and scary. Why did they want me in that bedroom?

I kept backing up; they kept approaching, all the time glancing uneasily toward my dark bedroom. As I got closer and closer to that dark bedroom I got more and more frightened.

Then, all of a sudden, I stopped, put my hands on my hips and said, *"Wait a minute! I don't have to be afraid of you! 'Greater is He who is in me than He who is in the world!' Watch this!"*

I turned toward the dark bedroom and said, *"In the name of Jesus I command the lights to come on!"* I snapped my fingers and the lights in my bedroom immediately came on!

I turned back to look at these hooded *"beings" a*nd watched in delight as they began screaming, *"Oh, no! Not that!"* I expected them to begin melting like the Wicked Witch in the Wizard of OZ, but instead, they just disappeared!

I awoke and sat straight up in bed. What in the world was that all about? I honestly believe that my message was to always put my trust in God and never fear whatever dark influences may be trying to attack me. **Thank You, Lord!**

Prior to the conversation I had with God in my bedroom, I had met a woman at church who was always saying things like, *"And I told the Lord...," "The Lord was telling me...," "While I was talking to God...."*

I used to think this woman was very strange! Talking to God! God talking to her! Who did she think she was? It wasn't until the incident in my bedroom when God spoke to me that I understood that ***ALL OF US CAN TALK TO GOD AND GOD WILL ALWAYS RESPOND!***

This woman told me that she had wanted to attend Bible School but her dad wouldn't pay for her tuition, so she just told God that she knew He would work it out for her to go...and sure enough, her father came through for her! She told me that while she was attending Bible School she found a little house in the neighborhood that she fell in love with and asked God to get it for her, and the owner ended up providing the financing so she could buy it!

She was always telling me these stories! It really started me thinking about some of the things that I wanted. Was it possible that I could ask God for help and He would do the same for me? Well, I was about to find out!

THE MIRACLE OF MY FIRST HOME

After my experience, or *"conversation with God,"* I began talking to God all the time, while I was getting ready in the morning, while I was driving my car, while I was shopping...everywhere I went I found myself carrying on a dialogue with God. Although it was a long time before I heard God speak out loud to me again, I definitely felt a *"presence"* with me at all times.

When I was about 29 or 30 years old, I was still unmarried, still out there taking care of myself, so I decided it was time for me to purchase a home. At that time I worked for a large residential homebuilder and saw people every day purchasing a home; why couldn't I purchase one also?

The homes we were building were a little too expensive for me, so I began my search for a home more within my price range. I spent every day checking out the want ads, then I spent every weekend driving around looking at homes for sale.

All to no avail.

When I found a home I liked, it was too expensive. When I found a home I could afford, it was in a bad neighborhood. Finally, one Sunday, about a month after I began my search, I came home and flopped down on my couch. I was exhausted and frustrated. Would I ever find a home?

All of a sudden it hit me. If my friend from church could ask God to get a home for her, why couldn't I ask

God to do the same for me? Hadn't I been talking to Him every day now for the past few months just as I talk to my other friends? Well, I let all of them know I wanted a home, why not tell God?

So I took a deep breath and said, *"Lord, I know You will help me find a home. To be specific, Lord, I would like a two-bedroom, not a three-bedroom home, since I don't need all that space. I would like to live close to my office, and I don't want to pay more than $35,000. If anyone can find it for me, YOU can! Thank You, Lord!* ***IT IS DONE!****"*

I ended my request with **"IT IS DONE"** because my friend from church said it all the time and when I questioned her about it she explained to me that saying **"IT IS DONE"** is acknowledging that since God will always give us the desires of our heart, we are thanking Him in advance, trusting that our prayer will be answered.

Praying for something and then saying **"IT IS DONE"** is akin to pressing the *"Start"* button on a fax machine. The prayer is automatically *"faxed"* and received instantly by God's *"staff"* — my guardian angels — who immediately set out to fulfill my request! Don't you love it?

I started visualizing my *"perfect"* home. I kept seeing a dining room with double windows that allowed lots of light to flow in. I could just see my beautiful emerald green luster with the cut-glass prisms that sat on my dining room table picking up the light from this window and reflecting off the walls.

I visualized the living room and bedrooms, and how I would arrange my furniture. I visualized the color of the

It Is Done!

carpet and the curtains I would put up. Son of a gun — I was actually *seeing* my little house already! I went to bed with a big smile on my face.

The next day I was sitting in a loan closing, which was part of the job I performed for the builder for whom I worked. At this particular closing there was also a Co-Op Realtor representing our buyers whom I knew from previous loan closings, so we sat there chatting while the Closing Attorney reviewed the paperwork with the buyers.

All of a sudden, the Realtor said to me, *"You won't believe the listing I got **YESTERDAY** for the cutest little house! It's a two-bedroom bungalow right around the corner! This house won't be on the market long; the sellers are only asking $32,000 for it!"*

I sat there with my mouth open! What? A two-bedroom house, close to my office, selling for $32,000? Wasn't that **EXACTLY** the description of the house I asked God to find for me just last night? Needless to say, I told this Realtor I wanted to go look at it the minute the loan closing was over!

The house was ten minutes from my office! The minute we pulled into the driveway, I fell in love with it. It was situated on a big corner lot with a lovely old oak tree right in the front yard.

We walked up the steps and he unlocked the door. As we walked into the living room, the sun was setting — *AND SUNLIGHT WAS FLOODING IN THROUGH*

THE DOUBLE WINDOWS IN THE DINING ROOM —
MY DINING ROOM!

I couldn't believe it! I didn't even ask God for the double windows, I just visualized them! And there they were! We wrote a contract on the house that very day and I went over to the mortgage company to fill out my loan application.

I was financing FHA, which meant that the FHA appraiser would have to report any deficiencies in the home that did not meet FHA minimum property standards.

Boy, did he ever report the deficiencies! The hot water heater had to be replaced. The kitchen floor had to be replaced. The carpet had to be replaced. The ancient heating system had to be replaced! (Forget air conditioning — this house was built in the '50s before air conditioning became standard!) The roof had to be replaced. The entire exterior had to be repainted!

Needless to say, the sellers were outraged! There was no way they were going to pay to have all of those repairs completed! I told them not to worry.

One of the benefits of an FHA loan at that time was that the borrower (me) was allowed to finance repairs not paid by the seller into the loan. And since I worked for a builder and knew a lot of subcontractors, I could take care of it! I would get the blue carpet I visualized. I could even have air conditioning installed, since it was a heating/air conditioning combination unit!

The cost of the repairs? $3,000. So how much did I pay for my little two-bedroom, practically like-new dream home? *$35,000 — **EXACTLY THE AMOUNT I TOLD GOD I COULD PAY!***

It wasn't until many years later that a friend gave me a book entitled *"Creative Visualization"* by Shakti Gawain. I was amazed to read in this book that whatever we visualize in our mind (our inner world) is what we can create in the **OUTER WORLD!** That was exactly what I did when I started *"seeing"* my home with the double windows in the dining room!

When I started decorating my home in my mind, arranging the furniture, hanging curtains, I had already accepted that **THE HOUSE WAS THERE!** So naturally I got my home **THE VERY NEXT DAY!**

Why did this miracle happen so quickly? Because I asked — **THEN ACCEPTED IT WAS MINE!** I have learned that when most people ask God for something, they won't leave it with God. They start worrying about it. They start doubting it will happen.

IF WHAT YOU THINK IS WHAT YOU GET, THEN YOU GET WHAT YOU THINK. WORRY AND DOUBT THAT IT <u>WON'T HAPPEN</u>, AND IT WON'T!

I believe that God tells us, *"When you pray for something, your prayer should **NOT** be a prayer of supplication, which means you don't believe you can have it, or you don't believe you deserve it. This is not a worthiness issue! Your prayer should be a prayer of **GRATITUDE**,* *accepting* ***IT IS ALREADY DONE — SINCE I WILL <u>ALWAYS</u> GIVE YOU THE DESIRES OF YOUR HEART!"***

I have also found that the more specific my request, the quicker my request is answered. This is one of the reasons I began writing down my desires.

I learned that I had to really focus on what I wanted before I could put it into words. The more I could focus on my desire, the quicker I received it. Try it!

THIS WAS MY FIRST BONA FIDE MIRACLE! I WAS ON MY WAY!

THE MIRACLE OF THE BOOKCASE

I closed the loan and then moved into my *"practically-new"* dream home and set about decorating it the way I wanted. I decided I needed shelves in my closet, so I went to The Home Depot and settled on an *"assemble it yourself"* particleboard bookcase.

The bookcase parts were all encased in a box which weighed a ton, but a Home Depot employee carried it out to my car and put in the trunk for me. I drove home, pulled into my driveway, raised the trunk lid and dragged the box out of my trunk. About the best I could do with that heavy box was stand it up and *"walk"* it up the sidewalk to my front door.

That's where I got stuck! There were five steps leading up to the door, and there was no way I could get that box up those steps!

I tried dragging it up. That didn't work, so I got on my back and with my feet I tried pushing it up! That didn't work either. I must have spent 15 minutes huffing and puffing over that heavy box! It just wouldn't budge!

In the meantime I was looking with concern at the black clouds that were forming in the sky. The wind was blowing and I smelled rain in the air! If I didn't get that box into the house before it began to rain, the water would ruin it! Wet particleboard is a disaster!

Finally, huffing and puffing, I sat down on the front porch steps and put my head in my hands. I couldn't do this. What was I going to do? It finally occurred to me to ask God to help me. I then said, *"God, You need to help me here! I'm not strong enough to do this! If I don't get this bookcase into the house before it starts to rain, it will be ruined! Please tell me what to do!"*

As I sat there quietly contemplating my dilemma I heard a voice say, *"Kathy, why don't you **OPEN THE BOX AND TAKE THE PIECES OUT ONE AT A TIME?"***

DUH! Boy did I feel dumb! Why didn't I think of that? I started laughing as I stood up to go get a knife to open the box. I said, *"Thank You so much, Lord! I don't know what I'd do without You!"*

It's so simple! I always have choices. When I reach a dilemma I can always do one of two things:

- I can run around like crazy and worry myself sick wondering what I'm going to do, then try to ***DO IT BY MYSELF, OR***

- I can ask God to help me, ***THEN LET IT GO AND TRUST THAT HE WILL HANDLE IT!***

Unfortunately, it seems that I must learn this lesson over and over again.

THE MIRACLE OF THE JOB INTERVIEW

I was now talking to God on a daily basis and asking Him for guidance and direction on everything, so when one of my girlfriends asked me to consider a position with the company for which she worked, I said OK, but asked God to tell me whether or not it would be a good move for me.

My girlfriend made arrangements for me to meet with her and the owners of the company one night at a local restaurant. As I pulled into the parking lot of the restaurant, I said to God, *"OK, Lord, here I go. I have no idea whether or not this job is right for me, but You do, so please let me know."*

As I pulled into a parking space, I noticed a car pulling up a couple of parking spaces over. A man got out of the car and began walking close behind me, but he picked up his step when he saw me.

He came along beside me with a big leering grin on his face **and began hustling me and making suggestive comments!**

I looked at this jerk with disgust and said, *"Get lost!"* He kept leering at me as he sailed past, entering the restaurant and disappearing into the crowd. I thought, *"Now there's a man who has a lot of respect for women!"*

My girlfriend was waiting for me as I entered. She said, *"Hey, there you are! You look great! Everybody's at a table in the back. Come on."* We started weaving our way through the crowd toward the table she pointed to and she said, *"We're back there, and it looks like Paul (or whatever his name was) is here, too. Let's go."*

I looked at the table she was leading me to and couldn't believe my eyes! Sitting there was **The Jerk** who made the suggestive comments to me in the parking lot! Oh, brother! So that was my potential new employer! I smiled and said under my breath, *"Thanks for the warning, Lord."*

We sat down and my girlfriend introduced me to the two men sitting there. **The Jerk** from the parking lot didn't bat an eye and showed no recognition for the woman he'd hustled in the parking lot. As a matter of fact, he was warm, cordial, and charming. If I hadn't seen **"the real person"** in action in the parking lot, I might have considered the job.

After the meeting I thanked them and told them I would consider the position. I got up to leave and my girlfriend jumped up, said her good nights to the two men, and followed me out to the parking lot.

As we walked toward my car she said, *"What's wrong, Kathy? You weren't your usual 'perky' self. Didn't you like them?"* What could I say? She worked for those guys. Of course, she'd only been with them about a month; maybe **The Jerk** hadn't shown his *"true colors,"* yet.

I stopped and related the incident in the parking lot. I was bewildered by her nonchalant response, *"Oh, that's just Paul's way; he doesn't mean anything by it."*

It Is Done!

I said, *"So he's come on to you?"*

She shrugged, *"Sure, but I know how to handle him."*

I asked, *"Doesn't it bother you that he treats you like a Bimbo instead of a professional? I could never work for a man like that. Respect is very important to me, and it's obvious that man has no respect for women."*

She said, *"Hey, it's a really good job and I'm making more money than I've ever made before. You gotta take the good with the bad."*

Not me! I didn't need any job that bad!

This was the attitude of a lot of women in the '70s. Women were beginning to make headway in the business world, but it generated massive fear among the men; strong women scared and threatened them!

The only way they could defend themselves was to launch an attack by making lewd and suggestive sexual comments to embarrass and demean them.

FEAR — it was all about fear. Whether it was the man who feared a woman would replace him, or a woman who refused to show someone else how to perform her job for fear she would be replaced, it all boiled down to the fact that they lived their lives in fear.

I should know; I lived with that fear up until my *"awakening."* This fear stems from a feeling of separation from God. God's *"up there"* and I'm *"down here."* The truth is, there is no separation. It's not about *"looking up"* for God; it's about *"looking within"* — *"I am with you always."*

When I developed a friendship with God, most of my fears diminished — not completely, of course, but quite a bit. I knew I was never alone and I trusted completely that God wanted all good things for me.

This feeling of aloneness that we experience when we don't know the **TRUE** God causes us to spend our life trying to be accepted by a group — any group; it doesn't matter which.

My heart goes out to those who succumb to *"peer pressure"* because of their desperate ache to *"be a part of the in-crowd."* Teenagers are especially susceptible to this pressure. Nothing is more important than *"being popular,"* and nothing is more devastating than *"not being part of the 'in-crowd'."*

As a teenager, I was considered *"an outcast"* because I wasn't pretty. It was so humiliating to have boys make fun of me; I still shudder when I think about it. I was a *"late bloomer"* and really didn't begin attracting men until I got out of high school.

Those were the years of the disco and I went with my girlfriends to all the local discos, where I fell in with the *"in-crowd"* in Atlanta and found myself being invited to all of the *"in-crowd"* functions. For the first time in my life I felt attractive and reveled in the attention.

It Is Done!

There were lots of drugs and marijuana being passed around in the '70s and '80s and someone was always trying to get me to try some.

I've always had a deathly fear of drugs and marijuana and had absolutely no desire to participate in any of that action. If I was at a function and saw someone pull out marijuana or cocaine, I left. I wasn't about to get caught in a raid! Drugs were illegal.

What I really did was turn a blind eye to what was going on — frankly, I compromised. At that time in my life being part of the *"in-crowd"* was more important, so I talked myself into believing that by leaving when drugs were produced, I was taking a stand against drugs. The truth was, I was too chicken to speak up because I was afraid they would kick me *"out of the clique."*

I avoided it as long as I could, but the pressure to *"indulge"* got heavy. Finally, I was pretty much given an ultimatum by one of the men in the group —*"Participate in the drugs and marijuana or don't participate with us at all."*

I was in a dilemma! For the first time in my life I felt I was *"accepted by the in-crowd,"* but I'd be kicked out if I didn't take the drugs — and become an *"outcast"* all over again. What to do?

I agonized for days, trying to decide. This was not an issue of *"committing a sin against God"* if I took the drugs; I wasn't afraid that God would punish me. What I did know, however, was that there are always conesquences to our actions and I just felt that I didn't want drugs messing up my mind or my body. (Yet I smoked; didn't I think cigarettes were messing up my body?)

I knew the right thing to do, but I kept remembering those terrible, lonely teenage years and shuddered at the thought of being alone again. I couldn't sleep that night; I kept tossing and turning.

Finally, I sat up in bed and said, *"Lord, please help me with this decision. I can't worry about it anymore!"* I turned out the light and fell asleep.

When I awoke the next morning, an interesting thought popped into my head, *"Well, Kathy, you survived your teenage years pretty intact; you'll survive this, too!"* Yeah, I would. I'd been alone before, I could handle it.

One of the advantages of being shunned and made fun of as a teenager is that when you become an adult you realize, if you can survive *that*, you can survive anything!

I made the decision. I just couldn't do it. I called this man back and told him the truth. *"I just can't do this,"* I said. *"I like spending time with you guys and enjoy the activities, but I don't want to be around when you're doing drugs. If it means I don't see you guys again, so be it."*

The response of my friend was, *"You don't know what you're missing, kiddo! See you around."* Oh well, what did I expect?

Then something really interesting happened. One of the girls in the *"group"* called to tell me that she heard about what happened and it started her thinking about *"the whole drug thing"* and she didn't want to do any drugs either! She said, *"You know, Kathy, most of us girls don't want anything to do with drugs. We just didn't have the guts to say 'no.'*

"I guess we kind of needed someone to make the first move. We've discussed it and decided that we're all going to tell the guys to cool it with the drugs. We're going out to celebrate — you've got to come!"

Gee, how about that? I thought I'd be alone again if I took a stand against drugs; instead I was accepted back into the fold with none of the pressure of doing something I didn't want to do!

The wonderful psychic, Edgar Cayce, summed it up best: *"An experience, then, is not only a happening, but what is the reaction in your own mind? What does it do to you to make your life, your habits, your relationship to others of a more helpful nature, with a more hopeful attitude?"*

There was a subtle change in my attitude toward these people after this incident and I found myself standing back and observing what was going on around me. Was this really where I wanted to be? Well, I thought it was!

My whole life's goal was to *"belong"* and now that I had achieved that goal I wasn't enjoying it anymore!

It wasn't that I was judging these people, it was just that I was searching for more meaning in my life, and this environment wasn't feeding that desire. I eventually drifted away from the group and never looked back. Maybe being part of the *"in-crowd"* wasn't so great after all, but I'm glad I had the chance to make that decision for myself.

THE MIRACLE OF TURNING FAILURE INTO TRIUMPH

Many people look at me with anger in their eyes when I tell them about my miracles. I know what they're thinking —*"Why does God answer **your** prayers when He doesn't answer **mine**?"*

The answer is quite simple. I have learned over the years that you can pray to God for help but no help will be forthcoming **UNTIL YOU TRULY RELEASE THE PROBLEM — AND LEAVE IT THERE!** Most of us pray for something, **THEN TRY TO HANDLE THE PROBLEM OURSELVES! WE WON'T LET IT GO!**

Since I am the original ***"Control Freak"*** I've had to learn this lesson over and over again!

Every time I try to handle a problem, it takes me ten times longer, with ten times more stress, than it would have if I had said immediately after a problem arises, *"Lord, I know there is a solution for the problem and I thank You for giving me the right answer."*

I still find myself falling into the trap, but I'm getting better! Now when a problem arises and I start worrying about what I'm going to do, I turn it over to God. When it comes into my mind again, I release it again...and again... and again.

The most difficult part of turning my problems over to God is the belief that I'm ***"copping out"*** if I don't deal with them myself. I have always believed that responsible people should handle their own problems, not expect someone else to take care of them. Besides, I always believed that God was too busy with the *"major problems"* to help me deal with my small problems!

I'm learning, however, that God never intended for this life I'm living to be a struggle.

If that were true, then why did Jesus say over and over again that we could do everything he did — if we only had the tiniest *"mustard seed"* faith?

Why *"wander in the wilderness of uncertainty"* when we can *"sail through the sea of tranquility?"*

CHOICES, CHOICES — WE ALWAYS COME BACK TO CHOICES!

I've learned over the years that whenever something is troubling me and I can't figure out what to do about it, before I go to bed at night I'll say to God, *"Lord, I know there is a solution for this problem and I know You have the answer. Thank You, Lord, for bringing this answer to me."*

When I wake up the next morning the answer always comes to me — ***AND SINCE IT'S FROM GOD I KNOW IT'S THE RIGHT ANSWER!*** Just like the situation I described earlier, when I couldn't sleep I turned my problem over to God and awoke with the answer.

But let's be clear on one issue: we are most definitely here on earth to learn and grow. *"Sailing through the sea of tranquility"* doesn't mean we don't encounter obstacles.

Remember, however, that obstacles in our life are put here for a reason.

I believe that obstacles occur in our life to allow us the opportunity to stretch to a higher level of accomplishment and self-esteem than we ever dreamed possible. Don't you feel really good about yourself when you overcome an obstacle?

The wonderful psychic and spiritual teacher, Sylvia Browne, tells us that the message she received from *The Other Side* is that we write our life plan ourselves when we are *Over There*, creating obstacles and situations here on earth in order for us to grow spiritually.

It kind of takes the fun out of our pity-party lament, *"Why me, Lord?"*

It puts the responsibility for dealing with life's challenges and obstacles squarely back on our shoulders, rather than placing the blame on some distant, unfair, unconcerned God *up there* who randomly throws us these curve balls just for the perverse pleasure of watching us squirm!

Although my many years of study and prayer have led me to totally agree with Sylvia Browne, that doesn't mean I always have to like it! It's so much easier to play a powerless victim than it is to deal with a negative situation! After all, if we *take responsibility*, then we have to *do something about it!*

I look back on the major obstacles in my life and I grudgingly have to admit that my biggest obstacles turned into my greatest triumphs. I can pat myself on the back now, but I still remember the fear and desperation I felt at the time. Many times I wondered why *"God had forsaken me!"*

I now recognize that my wonderful, loving God suffered every minute right along with me, but it's just like teaching your child to ride a bicycle.

You can only hold the handlebars for so long before you let them go and watch with fear as he wobbles and swerves and falls, gets up again and wobbles and swerves and falls...until he's no longer wobbling and swerving! He's riding the bicycle all by himself! Your heart swells with pride at what your child has accomplished!

That feeling of pride you feel for your child is nothing compared to the pride God feels for us when we overcome an obstacle! It's the *"Yes!" Factor! "Yes — I can do this!"*

You can't ride the bicycle for your child if he's ever going to learn for himself, and God can't solve your life's problems for you if you're ever going to grow spiritually.

Besides, you picked the obstacles — ***DEAL WITH THEM!***

Would you like to know a little secret? Here's the deal:

- As you grow spiritually and learn that God is guiding and directing you through the obstacles in your life, always there to advise you on the best solution to your problem, your fears diminish.

• The more your fears diminish, the easier it is to hear God speaking to you.

• The quicker you hear God speaking to you with the solution, the quicker you resolve the issue.

• ***IT'S THAT SIMPLE!***

Naturally I had to learn this lesson the hard way! After five years of working 80 hours a week for the builder I mentioned earlier, I decided to move from the management end of building into the selling end — I became an on-site sales agent for another large builder.

I figured if I was going to work that many hours a week I might as well get paid good money for it!

I picked the worst year in the history of housing to become an on-site sales agent! I hadn't been on the job even a month when interest rates started rising. I watched in bewilderment as the interest rates rose from 10% to 14% to 16% — all in about a three-month period! How was I supposed to sell houses with interest rates that high?

I spent those three months secluded in my model home with fear gnawing at my gut. How was I going to make money if I couldn't sell houses? How could I sell houses if interest rates were so high? Yeah, you're right — I fell into the ***"Pity-Party Trap!"***

Here was my dialogue with God: *"What's going on here, Lord? I only took this job because **YOU** told me when I prayed about it that it would be a good move for me. Did I hear You wrong? Are You playing games with me?"*

So I *"wandered in the wilderness of uncertainty"* for those three months, not exactly setting the world on fire with my home sales, not sleeping at night, unable to eat because my stomach was so upset. Believe me, I didn't hear God speaking to me at all! (Of course not; how could He? My mind was too cluttered with worry to take time to listen to Him!)

But I'm stubborn and pigheaded, and I truly believed that God **DID** give me the green light to take this job, so one night before I went to sleep I told God, *"Well, I don't get it, Lord, but You haven't steered me wrong yet, so I'm accepting that I'm where I'm supposed to be. Just show me what to do."*

Can you believe I wasted three months before I said that? Naturally, the minute I said it, things changed dramatically! I woke up the next morning feeling refreshed and totally convinced that everything was going to be OK.

That same day a young couple came into my model home to look around — ***for the third time!*** Instead of the usual habit I'd fallen into of commiserating with them on the outrageous interest rates, I stopped them before they walked out and said, *"You've been in here three times to look at this house; you know you want to buy it! So what's stopping you?"*

It Is Done!

I felt a little sorry for them — they looked like the proverbial *"deer caught in the headlights."* Their response was, *"We can't afford this house; just look at the interest rates!"*

I said, *"Forget rates, let's talk payment! If I can put you in this house at a payment you can afford, will you buy? Sit down and let me go through the numbers with you."*

They sat down and I pulled out a sheet of paper and wrote down exactly how much cash they would need to buy the home. Then I calculated the monthly mortgage payment they would pay and determined the monthly income they would need to earn to qualify for the loan.

I handed them the sheet of paper and they were stunned! They said, *"My gosh! Is that all the cash needed to get into this house? We have more than enough money! And we thought the monthly payment would be much higher than this! And our monthly income is more than this! Heck, yeah! If this is what it takes, we're ready to buy!"*

I couldn't believe it! Was that all it took? I jumped up and said, *"Let's go out and look at available lots."* I showed them the lots, they made their selection, and I wrote the sales contract that same day!

Was I ever proud of myself! I thought, *"Well, Lord, as usual You knew how to solve this problem! People talk about interest rates, but all they really care about is the monthly payment and the cash required to close! This is great!"*

I spent the rest of the day creating a sheet for each of the floor plans we offered, breaking down the three things I outlined for this young couple.

When I got home, I typed up the sheets and took them into the office the next day and ran copies.

Beginning that very day I included these sheets in the package of floor plans I passed out to the visitors to my model home. This incident occurred in November of 1981. In December of that year, ***I SOLD 25 HOMES! IN THE FIRST QUARTER OF 1982, I SOLD 42 HOMES, AND WITHIN 12 MONTHS I HAD SOLD ABOUT 162 HOMES!***

You should have heard the other on-site sales agents grumbling about my sales! *"Sure Kathy sold more homes than we did! She has the best model...She has the best location...She has...She has...She has..."* Yeah, sure guys. If you want to believe that, go right ahead. I tried to tell them why I sold so many homes, and I offered to give them the information, but they wouldn't hear it! They were too busy wallowing in envy and anger to take anything from me! After all, they were the *"pros"* while I was the *"new kid on the block!"*

Finally, the Sales Manager buckled under the pressure and moved me from *"the best location"* to *"the worst location."* This was an old subdivision that only had about 10 lots left to sell — ***all "dog" lots!***

I sold every one of them by calling up some of my old customers and telling them, *"You'd better hurry! These lots won't last long! There are only a few left! You'll never*

It Is Done!

*get a chance like this again, because the builder is offering **FANTASTIC DEALS!**"* I had all of them sold within a month or two!

THE MIRACLE ON THE EXPRESSWAY

One day when I was driving on the expressway to the subdivision where I worked, my car started sputtering and jerking — and then it stopped dead! I was horrified! Here I was on the expressway with cars whizzing past me at 70 miles an hour and my car just died! I looked in my rear view mirror with horror as a car came barreling toward me, then swerved to avoid plowing into me. I was in an absolute panic!

I looked at my gas gauge and it was sitting on empty! How could that be? I knew I had plenty of gas when I left my home! I've never run out of gas in my life; what was going on here?

I put on my emergency blinkers and opened my door to step out — and almost got my door knocked off by a speeding car!

I quickly slammed my door shut. Cars were swerving all over the place trying to avoid hitting me! I broke out in a cold sweat!

I knew if I didn't do something quickly I was going to get hit or killed! I put my hands on the steering wheel and said, *"God, You have to start my car. I don't know how I could have been so stupid to not notice I needed gas, but I'm here and I'm stuck. If You don't start my car I know I'm going to get killed!"*

It Is Done!

I took a deep breath and turned the key — *AND MY CAR IMMEDIATELY STARTED!* I breathed a sigh of relief and said, *"Thank You so much, Lord. I promise this won't happen again."* I drove up to the next exit and pulled into a service station to get gas.

This was in the days when attendants still pumped your gas for you, so I asked the attendant to fill it up. I watched out of my side mirror as he removed the nozzle and placed it in my gas tank. He stood there for a minute, then stopped and looked down at the ground. What was he doing?

I watched in bewilderment as he took the nozzle back out of my gas tank and hung it up, then he got down on his hands and knees and started peering up under my car. What in the world was this guy doing?

He finally stood up and came over to me and said, *"Lady, you have a **HOLE IN YOUR GAS TANK!** When I tried to pump gas into it, it poured out all over the ground. How in the world did you make it in here with no gas in your car?"*

I was stunned! A hole in my gas tank? Well, that certainly explained it! *"Oh Lord, thank You, thank You!"* I smiled at the attendant and said, *"It was a real miracle that I made it in here, wasn't it? Can you fix it for me?"*

The attendant assured me they could fix my car and gave me a ride to my subdivision. I sat there in my model home shaking my head in wonderment. I played the scene over and over in my mind.

How could I ever doubt that God will absolutely, positively answer every single prayer I make? He just started a car that had no gas in it! In the physical world, cars don't drive without gas. In the spiritual world, anything is possible!

While I was sitting there thinking about this incident, my Sales Manager came in and sat down. He looked at me and knew something was wrong. He said, *"What's the matter? You look funny."*

I related the incident of the past hour. When I finished telling him how I prayed to God to start my car, ***and it did***, he got a look of disbelief on his face and said, *"Come on, Kathy, you know God didn't start your car. Obviously you had gas in it."*

I said, *"But I had a hole in the gas tank — there was no gas in the car!"*

He rolled his eyes and said, *"There was gas in the car."*

Why argue? He didn't want to believe. We discussed his business and he left.

I shook my head after he left and said, *"Lord, now I understand why more people don't experience miracles in their life. If they don't believe, they don't receive."*

I told everybody I knew about my experience and watched with bewilderment as person after person rolled their eyes and said the same thing — *"Come on, Kathy, you know there was gas in your car!"*

It Is Done!

I didn't get it. All of these people were regular church goers. They read the Bible; they heard the sermons about miracles. Why didn't they believe miracles could happen to me or to them? Did they think miracles stopped when Jesus died?

This wasn't the only time I had a miracle on the expressway. A few years later when I was running my mortgage-training institute, I got a call from the owner of a mortgage company who wanted to talk to me about doing some training for his employees. We scheduled an appointment for the next day.

The next morning I went out to get in my car — *AND I HAD A FLAT TIRE!* I was so mad! I kicked the tire and went back inside to call the service station up the road to come and tow it in to fix the flat.

I called my appointment and explained what happened, and told him I would get there just as soon as possible. He wasn't very nice about it. I thought, *"Give me a break! I can't help that I had a flat tire!"*

After the service station tow truck towed in my car and fixed the flat, I got in and took off for my appointment. I was running about 45 minutes late and I was mad! I was banging the steering wheel while I barreled down the expressway grumbling, *"Why did I have to have a flat tire today? Why couldn't it happen when I didn't have an appointment? This could be a big fee for me! Now the guy's mad; maybe he won't want to do business with me now..."* and on and on!

When I finally shut up and calmed down a little, I smiled and said, *"Oh well, Lord, sometimes things can't be helped, right? I should be grateful that it didn't occur while I was driving on the expressway. Who knows? Maybe it kept me out of an accident!"*

All of a sudden I heard a voice speak to me, *"Kathy, this delay **did** keep you out of an accident!"* Wow! I almost wrecked my car from shock! I said, *"Thank You, Lord. When will I ever learn that putting every part of my life in Your hands means that I need to accept whatever comes along? How do You put up with me? I'm so sorry."*

As I drove toward my destination, traffic started slowing down. What was this about? Was there an accident? Oh yeah, there was an accident. The accident was ***ON THE EXIT RAMP I WOULD HAVE TAKEN TO GET TO MY APPOINTMENT!*** Police were directing traffic past the exit ramp and I was forced to drive to the next ramp to get off.

As I drove past that exit ramp, I looked in horror at the accident. A huge tractor-trailer evidently tried to get off at that exit and perhaps its brakes failed and the driver couldn't stop. Somehow that tractor-trailer ended up ***DIRECTLY ON TOP OF THE CAR IN FRONT OF IT! THEY WERE TRYING TO PULL A WOMAN'S BODY OUT OF THE CAR UNDERNEATH!***

Dear Lord in Heaven! I knew without a doubt that the woman in that car ***WOULD HAVE BEEN ME IF MY FLAT TIRE HADN'T DELAYED ME!*** I started shaking all over. I could hardly steer the car.

It Is Done!

I got off at the next exit ramp, found the office I was going to, pulled into the parking lot, turned off the engine — and fell apart! I couldn't stop shaking!

I felt so sorry for that woman and said a prayer for her and her loved ones. I knew that she was in very good hands on ***The Other Side***, but my heart went out to the loved ones who would miss her terribly. And once again I thanked God and my guardian angels for taking such good care of me.

How could I possibly live my life in fear when something like that happened? How could I not know that God was with me every second of every day?

On yet another occasion when I was driving home on the expressway late at night, as I came around a sharp curve headed toward an underpass I heard a voice very distinctly yell out, ***"Slow Down!"***

I immediately jerked my foot off the gas pedal. As my car began to slow down the car that was driving in the left lane next to my car ***began to swerve into my lane!***

I was forced off the road, but was able to come to a stop just before going into the underpass. If I hadn't slowed down that car would have pushed me directly into the wall of that underpass!

I breathed a sigh of relief and thanked God and my guardian angels once again for protecting me. Immediately this verse popped into my head: *"Yea though I walk through the valley of the shadow of death I will fear no evil — for Thou art with me!"*

I know one thing these incidents have taught me. Whenever there are delays while I'm driving, I don't get so angry anymore. I never know when that delay is keeping me out of an accident!

One of my girlfriends related an incident that happened to her one night while she was driving home. Suddenly, out of nowhere a car on the opposite side of the road came barreling directly toward her — this would be a head-on collision! She didn't have time to do anything but say, *"Oh Jesus, please help me!"*

She doesn't know what happened; it was as if that car actually **dematerialized and passed RIGHT THROUGH HER CAR!** It continued on behind her and ran right into a tree! She pulled over to the side of the road, shaking all over, and put her head on the steering wheel. She couldn't believe what had just happened. What exactly did happen?

She heard a siren and saw a police car speeding toward the accident. Boy, that was fast! Someone must have called the police.

When she realized they were taking care of the person in the car, she slowly pulled back onto the road and drove home.

When she was relating this story to me she was shaking her head in amazement. She still wasn't sure exactly what happened, but she told me that she knew without a doubt that she had witnessed a miracle.

THE MIRACLE OF MY NEW CAREER

I spent about three years working as an on-site sales agent. During that time a gentleman I knew from my days with my former employer would stop by to talk to me. This man was an FHA/VA inspector who handled inspecttions for the homes under construction in my subdivision.

He was also a developer, which is how I knew him. The builder I previously worked for purchased lots from him in a couple of his subdivisions, and since I handled all lot purchases we got to know each other pretty well.

He told me that he was developing a new subdivision and suggested that I think about becoming a builder and building in his subdivision.

He broached this subject on numerous occasions and I would always smile and tell him it was something to think about, although I never took it seriously.

It was during this time in my life that I met *"the love of my life."* Yeah, I fell in love and I fell hard. He lived in New York but came to Atlanta regularly on business.

As our relationship progressed we began discussing marriage and he said he was willing to move to Atlanta to be close to me. We got engaged and I put my house on the market, figuring it would sell pretty quickly.

But my house didn't sell; I couldn't understand it. It was a great little house, priced right, in a good location.

What was going on here? I asked God to sell it for me, but for some reason my prayers weren't working. That house was on the market for almost 90 days and I still didn't have any interested buyers!

One Sunday I rushed home from my on-site sales office all excited that the love of my life would be flying in that night, renting a car and driving to my house.

When he didn't show up, I started worrying. Where was he? Well, he never showed up. I spent a sleepless night wondering what happened.

Did he have an accident on the way to my house? Did his plane crash? Did he have an accident going to the airport in New York? You know the drill; we always think the worst has happened.

The first thing Monday morning when I knew his office would be open in New York, I called. Was Mr. — in, please? Yes, he was there. Well, at least I knew he hadn't been in an accident, but what happened?

When he got on the phone he was very cold and distant; what was this all about? He simply stated he was forced to cancel his trip and he would be in touch when he could re-schedule. Huh? This was my fiancé talking, not some stranger. Why was he acting so funny?

When he realized I wasn't going to let him off the hook, he asked me to hold on while he got up to shut his office door.

When he got back on the line he explained to me that his son — ***HIS SON?*** — had been hit by a car Saturday night and was in the hospital. I was stunned!

What son? He told me he was unmarried! As I listened in disbelief he began to stammer out the truth. ***He was married!*** His marriage was an unhappy one and he was in the process of negotiating with his wife for a divorce. Because of the legalities of dividing up the assets from his business and other assets, it was taking longer than he anticipated.

Now, with the injury of his son he felt he needed to stay in New York and see what happened. He didn't know when or if he would be able to see me again.

I hung up the phone in total shock. I was numb. How in the world could I have been so stupid and trusting? This happened to other people; not me. This guy went to church with me, for Heaven's sake! What a liar!

Monday was my day off, thank Heaven, because I knew there was no way I could have gone to work that day. I was devastated.

I never got out of bed that day. I never ate all day. I didn't take a bath, brush my teeth, comb my hair...I lay there hour after hour thinking about everything I knew about this man. I sure missed the signals.

After a sleepless night I dragged myself out of bed and tried to get ready for work. Fortunately I didn't have to be at my model home until 11 AM, so I dragged around getting myself together.

The thought of sitting in that model home all day, day after day, thinking about what happened made me sick at my stomach. How in the world was I ever going to get through each day? I knew that time would heal most of my wounds, but in the meantime all I could see for my future were the days just dragging out in front of me.

I sat down on the foot of my bed and talked to God. *"Lord, I don't know how I could have been so stupid, but it's over and done with. Now I have to get on with my life. I need Your help. I don't see how I'm going to make it sitting in that model home with my thoughts eating away at me.*

"Please help me. Keep me busy. Send people to my model home; send **SOMEONE OR SOMETHING** *to help me."* I took a deep breath, got up and drove to work.

That day happened to be one where my developer friend stopped by to say hello, and he started in again about my becoming a builder. I was in no mood for this, so I decided to cut him off, *"Mr. Clary, I don't know anything about being a builder! What makes you think I'd do that?"*

He said, *"Kathy, you know more about building than most builders. When you were with ABC Builders, you got all the development loans, you got all the construction loans, you purchased all the building permits, water meter permits, sewer taps, you handled the advertising, reviewed and signed all sales contracts, scheduled the closings, attended all the closings...in other words, Kathy, you did everything except supervise construction of the houses. And you don't need to know how to do that!*

It Is Done!

"All you need is a Construction Supervisor! I know a retired building inspector who would be interested in handling that for you — just pay him $1,500 for each house he supervises. You won't have to pay him until the loan closes."

He continued, *"I tell you what I'll do. If you're interested, I'll let you build in my new subdivision. I'll give you the lots and you won't have to pay me until you sell and close the house."*

What could I say? He had everything covered. I still resisted. *"It will take months to build and close a house! What am I supposed to live on until that time?"*

He said, *"Well, you know FHA and VA new construction loan guidelines better than anyone in this city! I do FHA and VA inspections for most of the large builders in Atlanta. I know I could talk to them about using you as a consultant. That'll give you some money to live on until your houses start closing."*

There you go. I was trapped. I said, *"I promise you I'll give it serious consideration. Give me a little time."*

After he left I talked to God, *"Well, Lord, is this the diversion I was praying for? Is this the right thing for me to do? Hmmm...how will I know? Well, I now understand why my house didn't sell before, so if this is the right thing for me to do, I'll know if You sell my house."*

The next day I had a contract on my house! I was trapped! What should I do? I decided that perhaps selling my house wasn't the right sign for me to quit my job and go out on my own; it would take more than that to make this decision, so I asked God to give me another sign. ***(Isn't it funny how we play games with God?)***

The next day I received a call from my Sales Manager asking me to come to his office. I drove from my model home to his office, went in and sat down. He got up and shut the door. When he sat down I could see that he felt really uncomfortable about what he had to say, so he took a deep breath and began.

*"The Home Office wants to make some changes. Apparently your commissions have been running substantially higher than they're used to paying **(WELL YEAH, I GUESS SO — I SOLD MORE HOMES FOR THEM THAN ANYONE IN THE COUNTRY!)**. They are changing your commission structure."*

That's all I heard. My company was cutting my commissions, despite the fact that I sold more homes for them than anybody in the country! While he continued talking, I tuned him out. Well, well, well...if ever there was a sign that it was time for me to move on, this was it! When he finished talking I said, *"I quit. I'll give you one month's notice. I've been thinking about it anyway. Mr. Clary has offered to get me started as a builder and I think I'll go for it."*

He wasn't surprised that I would quit. He thought the whole thing stunk and he couldn't believe they were doing this to me, but this idea of becoming a builder? Was I nuts? What did I know about building?

It Is Done!

He could get me a job as an on-site sales agent with another builder; wouldn't that be better for me than this crazy idea about becoming a builder?

Despite all of his attempts to dissuade me, my mind was made up. I was going to become a builder. I called Mr. Clary and told him I was ready to take the plunge. I had one month left with this company; could he call some of those builders for me about consulting work?

Mr. Clary was as good as his word. He put me in touch with some of the largest builders in Atlanta and I began doing consulting work for them, all the time working toward getting a place to live and establishing my building company.

I told the builders I was doing consulting work for that I was becoming a builder, and they laughed at me! You a builder? What do you know about building? I also ran into the builder I worked for previously at a Homebuilders Meeting and told him Mr. Clary was helping me become a builder. He laughed his head off! Kathy a builder? What an absurd idea!

So there I was, three weeks into my one-month notice, lying in bed one night unable to sleep! What in the world had I done? I sold my house, I quit my job, and I'm going to become a builder? Was I crazy? What ever made me think I could do this? I was actually becoming dizzy from a panic attack!

When I finally calmed down, I started talking to God. *"Well, Lord, I must tell You that I'm terrified of what I'm doing here! But I also believe from everything that happened to bring me to this point, that I asked for Your guidance, and You gave it. I have to believe that I'm doing the right thing. So I tell You, Lord, I'm giving all of my fear to You and I thank You for guiding and directing me."*

I decided to pick up my Bible and read a little bit of Psalms, as it always seemed to calm me. I just flipped the book open at random to Psalms and started at the top of the page. What I read stunned me!

It was Psalms 118, Verses 22 and 23: ***"The stone the builders rejected has become the capstone; the Lord has done this and it is marvelous in our eyes."***

I started laughing! Wow! Could God possibly have given me a more perfect verse to let me know that I was on the right track? What did I care what those other builders thought of my new career? The Lord was doing this for me!

I said, *"Oh Lord, You are so good to me! Thank You so much for giving me that confirmation! I'll never worry about it again!"*

I kept thinking about that word, *"capstone."* Since I felt very strongly that God had led me to that verse I decided to use the name for my building company — ***Capstone Construction.*** When I opened my mortgage-training institute a few years later, I used this name again — ***Capstone Institute of Mortgage Finance.***

This name has served as a wonderful witness to other people who ask me, *"Where did the name 'Capstone'*

It Is Done!

come from?" It allows me to share with them how God worked so wonderfully in my life!

THE MIRACLE OF MY FREE TRUCK

While trying to get my building company up and running, I realized that I was probably going to need a truck for the business. What to do? I didn't want to take cash out of my limited business funds to purchase a truck outright, and I certainly didn't want to begin my business in debt with a truck loan.

As I struggled with this issue, I remembered two people who had borrowed money from me over a period of about two years. One woman begged me for $1,000 that she needed for *"her sick aunt who needed an operation."* So I gave her the money (boy am I gullible!) only to find out later from a mutual friend that she used the money to buy a horse! Yes, a horse! She actually joked to our mutual friend about *"duping"* me with her sad story!

Another friend of mine who was always in trouble and always desperate for money borrowed over $3,000 from me over a period of two years. Like an idiot I helped him too! Altogether these two people owed me about $4,400.

The more I thought about these two people taking advantage of me, the madder I got! I kept thinking, *"It's not fair! If they would pay me the money they owed, then I could use it to buy a truck!"* I started having trouble sleeping at night, thinking about how those two people took advantage of me.

Finally, one night when I couldn't sleep — *AGAIN* — I began to pray to God about what I should do. While I

It Is Done!

poured out my heart to Him, moaning and groaning about how unfair it was, asking Him what I should do, He spoke to me and said, *"Kathy, forgive the debt, bless the debtor, and give it to Me."* Did I hear right, Lord? Forgive the debt and give it to You? How's that going to get my truck?

Once again He spoke to me, *"Trust me. Forgive the debt, bless the debtor, give it to Me and I'll take care of it."* I figured I had nothing to lose, so I replied, *"OK, Lord, I may not understand this but I'm going to forgive the debt, bless those two people, and give it to You and I'm trusting that You'll take care of me."*

You know, I slept better that night than I had in almost a month! From that point forward, whenever I thought about those two people who owed me money, I just said, *"Nope, I'm not worrying about this anymore, Lord! I've forgiven the debt, blessed those two and I trust that You're taking care of it!"*

About a month went by and I was attending a Homebuilders Association monthly meeting, where I met a man who wanted to talk to me about doing some consulting work for him. We left the meeting and stopped for a cup of coffee to discuss it. He told me he'd be in touch but I didn't feel I would hear from him again.

Two weeks later he called me. *"Oh good,"* I thought, *"He's calling to discuss some consulting work."*

While I sat holding the phone to my ear this man started *"hemming"* and *"hawing,"* cleared his throat, got silent, *"hemmed"* and *"hawed"* some more and finally said, *"Listen, I know this sounds a little bizarre, but by any chance **DO YOU NEED A TRUCK?**"*

I was stunned! I said, *"What?"*

He said, *"Well, I know this is a little unusual, but I'm a Deacon at my church. One of our members is a single mother whose son is very ill. I know she needs money for his medical expenses but she doesn't want to take charity from the church.*

*"We noticed that she posted a flyer on our church bulletin board for a truck she wants to sell. All of the Deacons and church leaders got together and decided to buy the truck, but we don't want her to know that the money is coming from us. We decided to find someone who is in need of a truck and give them the money to buy it. **AND I DON'T KNOW WHY, BUT YOUR NAME JUST POPPED INTO MY MIND.**"*

I was speechless! I couldn't believe what I was hearing! I replied, *"Well, as a matter of fact, I do need a truck. I've just started my building company and was wondering how I would be able to afford a truck."*

He said, *"Well, if we give you the money you must promise not to tell this lady that it came from the church. Is that OK? She's asking $4,400 for the truck. I'll make arrangements to get you a check."*

I said, *"How much did you say she's asking for the truck? Did you say $4,400?"* ***I ABSOLUTELY, POSITIVELY FELT LIKE I HAD BEEN STRUCK BY LIGHTNING! $4,400! THAT WAS <u>EXACTLY</u> THE***

AMOUNT OF MONEY THOSE TWO PEOPLE OWED ME!

The man asked if I was all right and I assured him that I was fine; I was just amazed that they were willing to do this for me!

I got off the phone and sat there thinking about what just happened. I knew without a doubt that God did this.

I found it interesting that the price of the truck — $4,400 — was exactly the amount those two people owed me. I got the feeling that God was trying to teach me something here! So I ended up with a *free truck!*

I never heard from the man who owed me money, but I did run into the woman at a social gathering at least *six years* after this incident. When she walked in the door and saw me standing there, the blood drained from her face, she whirled around, almost knocked two people down, and took off running out the door! I cracked up! I've never seen anything so funny in my life! She looked like she'd seen a ghost!

I said, *"Oh Lord, she doesn't understand, does she? All these years she's known that she owed me money and has never made any attempt to pay me! All of these years she's lived in FEAR of being confronted by me! She doesn't understand how her negative actions are blocking Your wonderful blessings! Please, Lord, help her to understand."*

I remembered reading in the Bible that we should forgive those who have wronged us and bless them, rather than curse them. Well, I used to believe that this was a pretty stupid teaching! Bless those who wronged me? Give me a break! Now, of course, I understand that harboring hatred and anger against another works as a *"wall"* to prevent God's blessings from reaching us.

I've also learned that there is a very real ***"Law of Cause and Effect"— "What goes around comes around."*** This law is immutable; it never changes. It either works ***For*** you — *"Do good and good comes back to you"* — or ***Against*** you — *"Do bad and bad comes back to you."*

Forget pursuing legal action — ***GIVE IT TO GOD!***

THE MIRACLE OF COLLECTING ON A DEBT

The suggestion of *"Giving it to God"* was never truer than for my friend Rebecca. Rebecca is a brilliant woman with many talents and abilities. I received a call last year from an attorney with a law firm in Mississippi that was representing a mortgage company being sued by one of their borrowers. They called me to see if I could help them find a particular *"expert witness"* to help them defend the suit.

The more the attorney described the person they were looking for, the more it sounded like my friend Rebecca, so I recommended her. I told them I would call her to see if she was interested. When I called her and related their needs, she became very excited and said she'd follow up with them.

She got the job! She spent about four months traveling all over the country gathering data for them. Because of the material she put together and because of her *"expert witness"* testimony, they won the lawsuit!

She stopped by to see me a couple of months ago and I asked her about the lawsuit. She described what she did for them and told me how her testimony, combined with the information she compiled for them, pretty much guaranteed they would win, but there was one little problem — ***THEY WOULDN'T PAY HER!***

She scrounged around in her briefcase and pulled out the invoice she had sent them, which included not only payment for her time but reimbursement for her extensive travel expenses — money she had paid out of her own pocket. They owed her *over $15,000!* She had been trying to collect from them for *months* and they just refused to pay!

I told her I felt terrible! After all, it was I who recommended her for the job! She said, *"Don't worry about it, Kathy. I appreciate your thinking of me and I'm glad I had the opportunity to do this kind of work. I guess I'll have to hire an attorney and pursue it through the courts."*

I said, *"Before you do that, let me see that bill."* I took the bill and laid it on my desk and told Rebecca to put her hand on it. I then placed my hand on top of hers and said, *"Lord, we know all blessings come from You.*

"For whatever reason these people haven't paid, we release it and bless them. We know You are our source and we know You will provide. We thank You, Lord, for always taking such good care of us. IT IS DONE!"

I handed the bill back to Rebecca and said, *"There is no better place to put this debt, Rebecca. Trust me — something will happen."* Rebecca is a believer, so she agreed to let it go.

About a week later, one of my employees brought me a fax — from Rebecca — *IT WAS A COPY OF THE $15,000+ CHECK SHE HAD RECEIVED FROM THE LAW FIRM IN MISSISSIPPI!* Scrawled across the fax was Rebecca's note: *"See, Kathy? Miracles really work! Bless you!"*

THE MIRACLE OF THE LOST RING

Remembering Rebecca's story reminded me of another incident that occurred a couple of years ago. My husband and I joined a health club here in our building and started going to work out a few mornings a week before coming in to the office.

I would always remove my jewelry and place it in a locker in the Ladies' Locker Room, lock it with my padlock and go to work out. On one particular day after working out, I opened my locker and removed my towel to go take a shower.

As I was standing under the shower it hit me — *"I forgot to put the padlock back on my locker! Oh no! My wedding ring and other ring and watch are in there!"* I hurriedly stepped out of the shower, dried off, and went rushing back to my locker.

As I opened the door and started looking through my things, my heart fell. Thank God my wedding ring and watch were still there, as was all the money in my wallet, but my other ring was missing!

I walked all over that room thinking perhaps that I dropped it somewhere. I also asked all of the ladies in the room if they had seen it, but nobody knew anything about it. It was gone.

I sat down on a bench, very, very disappointed and dejected. That particular ring meant a lot to me. It was one that I had a jeweler design for me that contained a large lapis lazuli blue stone and about 30 Pave′ diamonds set in both yellow and white gold. I couldn't believe it was gone!

I took a deep breath and said, *"Oh well, Lord, after all I've been through these past few years, I realize this ring is only a 'thing;' it's not important. I don't know what happened to it; I don't know if someone took it or what. If they did, then I bless them, I bless the ring, and I release it to You. There is nothing in this world that I can't live without, Lord, except You."*

When I met my husband in the lobby and told him what happened, he was outraged! He wanted me to call the police! I said, *"No, honey, it's OK. If someone took it, let them have it. It's not that important to me."* I went to the desk and told the clerk that I had lost a ring; could I fill out a little post card and post it on the bulletin board?

I filled out the card, describing my 'lost' ring and stuck it on the bulletin board — and forgot all about it.

More than ***three months later*** my husband and I walked into the health club and the clerk at the desk looked up. When he saw me, he motioned for me to come over. I walked over to the desk and he said, *"Aren't you the lady who lost the ring with the blue stone in it awhile back?"* I nodded my head, yes. He said, *"Well someone turned it in yesterday."* He opened a drawer behind the desk — **AND PULLED OUT MY BEAUTIFUL LAPIS AND DIAMOND RING! I COULDN'T BELIEVE IT!**

I looked at my husband and said, *"You see why I didn't call the police, honey? If I had, I would have never seen this ring again. Instead, I gave it to God and He brought it back to me!"*

Can you imagine this ring turning up over three months later? I have no idea what happened to that ring, and I don't care. I let it go. All I know is that this was just one more miracle that God brought into my life!

Another lesson I have learned over the years is that we are here to *enjoy* all of the beautiful things in the world, including beautiful clothes, beautiful jewelry, beautiful cars, homes... whatever. And we deserve all of these things. However, they are here for us to ***ENJOY, NOT POSSESS.*** The more we endeavor to possess *"things"* the more we fear we will lose them. They are *"just things!"* Don't waste time worrying about losing them!

You never *"own"* anything. Trust me.

So relax — enjoy them while you have them, but don't worry about losing them. Besides, even if you do lose them, just let them go and trust that there is plenty more where that came from — ***AND YOU AUTOMATICALLY ATTRACT PLENTY MORE!***

We can walk through a beautiful garden and enjoy God's magnificent flowers, with their wonderful varied colors and sweet smell, there for everyone to enjoy. But if we pick one of the flowers and *"possess"* it, it dies. The beautiful color and wonderful smell is destroyed.

Everything we think we *"own"* is really just a temporary *"gift"* from God. The easier we can enjoy the gift and release it, the easier we will receive more gifts. It's the boomerang effect — throw it out there and watch it come back to you!

I START MY NEW CAREER

I started my building company and began construction on a few houses. I also consulted for a couple of large building companies in Atlanta. While I was consulting for one of these building companies, I got to know the Manager pretty well and we began dating. I was still nursing my broken heart so it helped to pass the time.

After dating for almost a year we decided to get married. Did I love him? I don't really think I did. I think I reasoned that I would never feel for another man what I felt for my former love, but at least this man treated me well and we had the building business in common. (Boy do we sometimes pick dumb reasons to marry!)

Another thing that swayed me toward marrying him was a story he related to me. He was with me one day when I pulled out my checkbook to write a check for something.

While I was writing the check, I noticed him staring at it; what was going on here? I asked him about it later, but he just shrugged it off and said he remembered something while I was writing the check; it wasn't important.

When he asked me to marry him, he told me the significance of the incident with the check. A few months before he met me, he was very depressed. His second marriage had failed two years before and he was feeling very alone. All he did was go to work and go home; nothing brought him any joy or satisfaction.

One night, out of desperation, he took a whole bottle of sleeping pills — and died. He made the trip down the "tunnel" that so many people who've had a "near-death" experience talk about, and he came out into a beautiful white light.

In this light he saw a beautiful being and poured his heart out to him, telling him about his loneliness and discouragement.

When he finished, this beautiful being spoke to him, saying, *"I understand your pain and I know how difficult it is for you, but it's not your time yet. You must go back. But I'm not sending you back alone — I'm sending someone to help you."*

He said he felt himself being whooshed back down the tunnel, but as he was leaving he saw three very distinct letters in front of him —**"KAL."** He came to in his bedroom and made a mad dash for the bathroom, where he immediately regurgitated the sleeping pills. Ever since that incident he kept wondering what the word **"KAL"** meant. Then, when he saw the name on my checkbook, **"Kathleen A. Lewis"** — **"KAL,"** he just knew I was the person God had promised to send to help him. Would I marry him?

How do you respond to a story like that? Was this my mission, to help this man? I did ask God if this marriage was right for me, and asked Him to show me if it wasn't. No answer was forthcoming, so I went ahead with it.

This man who had treated me so great before we got married literally changed from Dr. Jekyll to Mr. Hyde beginning the day after our wedding! I stayed with him for five miserable years because I thought I could help him! Brother, anybody who thinks you can help another human being who doesn't want to be helped is living in total denial!

Neither God nor you can help anyone who doesn't want to be helped. It's hard to finally realize that there are certain people out there who just like being miserable! It was not a happy time for me.

I realized that God may have very well sent me to help this man, but he wasn't willing to do anything to help himself!

Miracles were still happening to me, though. Thank Heaven I didn't let him interfere with my relationship with God! Before we married he applauded my *"talking to God."* After we married, he mocked it. Deep down I think he was jealous that I had this *"pipeline to God."* I kept trying to tell him that he did too, but he didn't want to hear it.

For years after the horrible experience of that bad marriage I asked God why He let me go through with it. What was that ***"KAL"*** all about?

What I realized is that we never seem to learn the tough spiritual lessons, like forgiveness, releasing judgment, or tolerance, unless we experience situations that force us to confront these very issues. It wasn't until many years later that I understood why this man was brought into my life.

I think his biggest problem was that he didn't like himself very much and didn't feel worthy in God's eyes, therefore he couldn't possibly ask God for anything. Like worthiness has anything to do with it! It stemmed from his childhood, of course, where he was told all of his life what a *"nothing"* he was.

Oh well — he wrote his life plan on ***The Other Side.*** He picked the situations to experience and learn from, and hopefully he'll learn them.

A few months after we married he decided to quit his job and take over my building company, since I *"didn't have a clue about the right way to run it."*

This man was practically a genius when it came to anything involving construction and he certainly did a wonderful job with the previous builder, so I decided our best route would be to find a piece of property and develop our own subdivision.

I sat down at my typewriter and typed a letter to God: *"Lord, I believe we can develop our own subdivision and I believe the right location and the right piece of property is here for us right now! I ask You to guide me in finding this property. Thank You, Lord!* ***IT IS DONE!"***

When I broached the subject with my husband, his response was, *"There's no way you'll be able to do this! We don't have any money to buy the property and no bank is going to give us a development loan without prior experience, so just forget it!"*

It Is Done!

I had made up my mind that it **COULD** work and I wouldn't be dissuaded so I started scouring the Sunday classifieds under *"Subdivision Lots and Land."* It wasn't a week or two later that I noticed an ad for a piece of property located in the county in which we were currently building so I decided to call.

I made arrangements to meet the Realtor at the property and knew immediately it would be a great location for a subdivision. It was located on a main road and had water availability, which would cut down on development costs. It was also less than a mile from a local elementary school. Perfect!

As I walked the land with the Realtor, I asked questions about the property owner, trying to get a feel for whether or not the owner would be willing to work with me on a joint venture.

It turned out that the property was owned by an individual free and clear, and had been in his family for years. Perfect! I wouldn't have to mess with a big corporation!

I asked the Realtor if perhaps the landowner would be interested in doing a joint venture with me on the development, making substantially more money in the long run than just the sales price of the land. He looked at me like I was nuts and said (in a condescending manner) he didn't believe the landowner would be interested. My reply was, *"It won't hurt to ask, will it?"*

After convincing the Realtor that it was a better deal for the landowner and urging him to ask, he reluctantly agreed to present the offer to the landowner. To the Realtor's great surprise, the landowner was interested! I met with him and presented my suggestion that we do a joint venture.

If he sold the land outright he would make $—, but he would then have to pay capital gains tax on that money.

If he did a joint venture with me, he would profit from each developed lot that we built on, so at the end of two years he would **TRIPLE THE MONEY HE WOULD MAKE BY SIMPLY SELLING THE LAND!** Also, he wouldn't be paying a huge portion of his profit for capital gains taxes.

He really liked the idea! He said he would get back with me, and proceeded to do a thorough background check on me (all my business associates called to tell me he had been in touch with them), requesting a copy of my credit report (fortunately I had impeccable credit and no debts). Finally, he made the decision to go for it!

The whole time these negotiations were progressing, my husband was telling me:

"You'll never be able to find a piece of land in the location we want!" He was stunned when I found it within a couple of weeks.

"You'll never be able to put together a deal to buy the land!" He was shocked that the landowner agreed to do a joint venture!

It Is Done!

"You'll never be able to find a bank to give you the development loan!" He was extremely shocked when a local bank agreed to do the development loan!

I now had my own subdivision! I was so excited I could hardly sleep at night thinking about all the steps involved in developing a subdivision. Since my husband had the necessary equipment down on his horse farm to handle the grading and development, I agreed to let him handle it. ***BIG MISTAKE!***

I watched in horror and dismay as the entire project fell apart. My husband's equipment constantly broke down. He managed to anger and alienate every single County official that came out to inspect the work in progress, resulting in turn-downs and more delays. He couldn't get along with the subcontractors. One delay after another occurred...week after week...month after month... until I was finally forced to throw in the towel.

I ended up giving the land back to the owner, who proceeded to develop it and sell the lots to other builders. My dream died.

I guess I could have taken the project away from him and given it to another crew, but I stupidly kept thinking my positive attitude would prevail.

When someone is hell-bent on failure, however, it's very difficult to overcome that attitude, and I believe my husband was envious of the ease with which the project came together and subconsciously set out to destroy it.

In my efforts to hold our marriage together I let my business fall away, and I realized we couldn't work together, so I spent a great many sleepless nights asking God to help me find something else to do. Once again I received an answer immediately. I was about to embark on a new career!

THE MIRACLE OF MY THIRD NEW CAREER

The two large building companies for whom I consulted were having difficulty dealing with the mortgage companies that were handling the financing for their buyers. Most of their buyers were financing FHA or VA, and FHA/VA new construction requirements could be very complicated. However, that was my area of expertise.

The Managers of these two large companies ran into each other one night at a monthly Homebuilders Association meeting and started commiserating with each other about the problems they were having with their mortgage companies. They both agreed, however, that they were glad I was helping them deal with their FHA/VA problems.

The more they talked, the more I came into the conversation. One of them laughed and said, *"If Kathy were handling our loans, we wouldn't be having these problems with the mortgage company!"*

He stopped and they looked at each other and both spoke in unison, *"Well, why **can't** she handle our loans? Why don't we get together and call her to see if she's interested?"*

Once again, God answered my prayer! I received a call from one of these two men asking for a meeting. I thought it was pretty strange that two large builders, really competitors, wanted to meet together with me, but I agreed to the meeting.

When they laid out their idea to me, I immediately saw the possibilities. Why not take on their loans? I'd been in and around the mortgage business for years; I could do this. I figured what I didn't know about the mortgage business I could learn.

I suggested that I go to work for the mortgage company that handled the loans for my old builder, since that lender knew me, so together we placed a conference call to the owner of that mortgage company to discuss it.

After explaining what we wanted to do, the mortgage company owner enthusiastically agreed — why wouldn't he? We were bringing at least $2 million in monthly business to his company!

When I told my husband what I was going to do, he hit the ceiling! How could I do this to him? He needed me to help him! How was he going to handle the building company alone...and on and on. There was no way I could continue to work with him, and I knew if the marriage was to be salvaged I needed to distance myself from the business end of our relationship, so I calmly stated, *"You'll do just fine,"* and started my new career.

What actually happened was that I walked into total chaos! Never in my life had I seen a business run like the mortgage business! Nobody knew anything! Nobody had time to teach me anything!

The only person who did know was the Underwriter — and she wasn't talking! That sign on her door **"DO NOT DISTURB"** infuriated me! How were we supposed to do our job if she wouldn't help us?

It Is Done!

I waited for her to go home at night, went into her office, took her underwriting guidelines books, and started photocopying them...night after night until I had my own set of books.

The only good thing about my job was that it kept me busy 80 hours a week so I didn't have to deal with my husband — plus I was making very good money.

My husband had a 26-acre horse farm, about 50 miles away from our home, that he had been renting out since his last divorce some three years ago. The tenants were having problems with the well and he was spending a lot of time down there trying to correct the problem. He was obnoxious and verbally abusive to me but not physically abusive...until one incident occurred that made me take some steps to get out of this relationship.

One Saturday he had to go down to the farm to fix yet another problem and he wanted me to finish painting the vaulted ceiling in the living room of our new house while he was gone. I looked at that vaulted ceiling **way up there**, looked at what seemed like an 800-foot ladder I would have to climb up, gulped, and said, *"I don't think this is something I'll be able to do."*

His face turned red with rage and he stormed out the door, yelling, *"You're useless! You're no good for anything!"* By that time I was used to the verbal abuse, but what he did next was just too much. As he walked by me he took his arm and knocked me aside, into a table. He didn't look back to see if he hurt me; he stormed out to his car and took off.

I fell into the table, which collapsed on top of me, and hit me in the head. I saw stars. That was it. My parents never physically abused us kids; they always talked to us with kindness and respect. I didn't have to take this anymore!

I went into the bedroom and started packing. I was still packing when he came home. He wanted to know what I was doing. I told him, *"Absolutely, positively, under no circumstances will I ever allow you to lay a hand on me again! I'm out of here!"*

We had only been married about seven months and I felt like I'd been married for years!

Then came the tears, the apologies, and the remorse. He was so sorry. He was under a lot of pressure. He never meant to hurt me. He didn't realize he knocked me so hard. It would never happen again...and on and on.

I looked at him and said, *"You need help. You can't control that horrible temper of yours. I can't deal with your depression anymore. I refuse to live like this; life is too short!"*

He begged me to stay. He promised he would get professional help. Then he told me that what he really wanted to do was sell our brand new home and move back to the horse farm.

His tenants were moving out. He knew if he were there he could fix all the problems on the farm. Besides, a friend of his had just completed a new subdivision in that county and offered to sell us the lots to build on. He just knew that

It Is Done!

if he could get back to his farm and build in that new subdivision, everything would be OK. Could I please give him another chance?

So I stayed, probably because I didn't want to admit to my friends and family what a horrible mistake I had made. I agreed to allow him to move back to the house on his farm and I would stay in our new home and put it up for sale. I knew this meant that I would now be responsible for all the bills...two mortgage payments, two sets of utility bills, car payments, etc., but I was making good money at the mortgage company and figured I could handle it.

He moved to the farm and I lived alone in our new home in peace and quiet and we saw very little of each other for about 30 days. But I wasn't happy with my new career.

While I was making good money, I was running myself ragged, had lost about 17 pounds, and all of the blood vessels on my shoulders had burst from stress; this wasn't working.

One night I was sitting alone at the kitchen table looking at my paycheck for the month. While I grossed over $8,000 that month, I only netted about $5,000. I took out my calculator and figured the number of hours I worked each week to earn that $5,000, and I discovered I was making about $15.00 per hour! I just couldn't do this anymore!

I had no idea what to do. I knew I didn't want to work with my husband, and I knew I didn't want to go back to being an on-site sales agent; what to do? I said, *"Lord, I'm* *so grateful to You for bringing this new career to me and for everything I've learned, but I just can't do this anymore. I have no idea what I should do, but **YOU DO!** Please help me find something new to do."*

I took a deep breath, sighed, and went to bed.

It Is Done!

THE MIRACLE OF MY FOURTH NEW CAREER

About a week after my talk with God I received a phone call from a Realtor who was in a panic. She had just lucked into a new listing agreement with a builder to sell the homes in his new subdivision. The problem was, she knew nothing about new home sales! While she was panicking and wondering how she was going to pull this off, she said, *"Your name just popped into my head! You're kind of a legend in this city, Kathy. You sold more homes in a year than anyone I've ever known.* **Have you ever thought about teaching a class to Realtors about on-site subdivision sales?"**

I laughed and said, *"Teach? I've never taught anything in my life! I don't know how to teach!"*

She said, *"I think there would be a real market for this class. I know tons of Realtors who would be interested. Why don't you think about it? I'll help get people to sign up for it, and do anything I can to help promote the class."*

I laughed and said, *"I don't have the slightest idea how to go about creating a class or writing a book for it! I couldn't possibly do this!"*

After pleading with me some more, I promised her that I would think about it. I hung up the phone and started laughing. How ridiculous! Me teach? I didn't have the slightest idea of how to go about this; what made her think I could ever teach...and then I stopped dead.

I said, *"Lord, is this You? Is this the answer to my prayer? But teach, Lord, I don't know..."*

The more I thought about it, the more it appealed to me. Teach, huh. And teach something I know so well. Hmmm...

"Lord, how will I know if this is You? Well, I guess if I could make as much money teaching as I could originating mortgages, that would be a pretty good indication that it's You. I don't know, I'm making about $5,000 a month after taxes now. Could I possibly make that much money teaching?"

I went to bed with my head full of ideas. Maybe, just maybe I could do this...When I awoke I made up my mind. I'd try one class. If I could make as much money teaching as I could originating mortgages, then I knew it was the right move for me.

I decided to take a *"leap in faith."* I sat down and wrote out a general outline for the course and what would be covered. Then I made arrangements with a local hotel to hold the class in their facility, prepared a flyer advertising a one-day class, **"Specialized Training for On-Site Subdivision Sales,"** with a fee of $50 per person, and had it distributed through a local flyer service to all the Real Estate companies in Atlanta. I waited for the response.

I don't really know what I expected, but I certainly didn't expect the overwhelming response I got! The hotel room would hold up to 100 people — **but more than 100 Realtors signed up for the course!** And still the registrations kept coming in! I had to cut the class off at 100 people but went ahead and scheduled a second class to handle the overflow!

Of course, now that I had the people signed up, I had to sit down and write the course! I suppose I went about this backwards — I probably should have written the course and the book ***BEFORE*** I advertised the class, but the positive response actually gave me the inspiration to sit down and write it.

I discovered that it came pretty easily for me! With *"God as my co-pilot"* the words just flowed! Since I had spent five years working for a major builder behind the scenes before becoming an on-site sales agent, that added experience allowed me to include tons of valuable information that every good on-site agent needed to know in order to be successful.

The first class was a huge success and word started getting around about the class. My phone was ringing off the hook with inquiries from Realtors wanting to know when the class would be offered again! The second class filled up quickly and I started taking reservations for a third class!

I was overwhelmed! Once again, God came through for me! I had my answer! I had told God if I could earn as much money doing this as I could originating mortgages, I would move in this direction. The figure I had in mind was $5,000 — ***I MADE THAT MUCH IN ONE DAY WITH MY FIRST CLASS! AND I ALREADY HAD A SECOND CLASS BOOKED AND A THIRD CLASS ON THE WAY! WOW! TALK ABOUT CONFIRMATION FROM GOD!***

This was all it took for me to make my decision. I quit my job. ***GOD HAD NEVER STEERED ME WRONG, AND I KNEW HE WOULDN'T STEER ME WRONG THIS TIME!*** This felt right to me and I had total faith that God would continue to provide.

I agreed to stay on at the mortgage company until they could find someone to replace me, and I assured the two builders that I would continue to offer consulting support just as I had in the past. I just explained that handling mortgages *"wasn't my bag."* They weren't happy about it, but I made sure I was replaced by a good Loan Officer and I taught her everything I knew. I was ready to move on.

Within a 30-day period I taught my course twice and scheduled a third class for the following month. Was I worried about where my next dollar would come from? Nah.

I'm a hard worker and I knew I could always do something to make money — besides, I knew that God was taking very good care of me!

Sure enough, shortly after I taught this second class for Realtors I received a call from a local bank. They were putting together a loan processing class for their employees and someone gave them my name as a candidate to teach the class. Would I be interested? So I met with them and agreed to teach this class.

I should point out that this bank had no idea I had left the mortgage industry and was teaching a class for Realtors.

Just like the incident where the truck was given to me ***BECAUSE MY NAME POPPED INTO THAT MAN'S HEAD,*** this bank called me ***BECAUSE MY NAME CAME UP!*** Where did this come from? ***FROM GOD, OF COURSE! IT'S REALLY THAT EASY!***

If I was born with one gift, I would say it was the gift of faith. And it's that gift of faith that opens the floodgates for the flow of wonderful things in my life. I don't live my life in fear.

When I pray to God and ask Him for something ***I BELIEVE IT'S MINE AND I RECEIVE IT.***

Most people ask God for something, then fear they won't get it. Since your thoughts dictate the "things" you manifest, your prayer isn't answered. Rather than the old saying, *"you'll **believe** it when you **see** it,"* I love the title of one of Wayne Dyer's books, *"You'll **See** It When You **Believe** It."*

Miracles would happen every day in everyone's life if they believed they would receive them.

I taught my class to Realtors for a few months as well as the loan processing class, all the time bringing in at least $5,000 per month, just as I had asked God to provide.

THE MIRACLE OF THE RED DRESS

I was always active in our local Homebuilders Association and attended meetings on a regular basis. I knew many people in the building industry and was always serving on several committees with the Association.

I was very flattered when they asked me to serve as a presenter for their annual Awards Banquet, but my joy was short-lived — ***WHAT WAS I GOING TO WEAR? I HAD A CLOSET FULL OF CLOTHES BUT NOTHING WAS SUITABLE FOR THIS FUNCTION! I HAD TO FIND A DRESS AND I HAD ONE DAY TO DO IT!***

I kid you not when I tell you I got up early on a Saturday morning and arrived at the local mall just as the doors were opening! I walked through every single shop looking for the perfect dress! No luck!

I drove to a second mall and walked through every shop looking for the perfect dress. No luck!

I drove to a third mall...and a fourth mall...and a fifth mall! I used up half a tank of gas and spent the entire day looking for that dress — with no luck! The last mall was more than 50 miles from my house and I was getting desperate! What was I going to do? I had depleted all avenues; there was nowhere else to go!

Finally, after wandering all over that fifth mall with no luck, I was exhausted! I dragged myself over to a bench and sat down. I was so discouraged. Then an idea came to me — why didn't I ask God to find my dress? ***WHY DIDN'T I DO THAT IN THE FIRST PLACE?***

So I said, *"God, please find my perfect dress. And here's what I want it to look like."* I shut my eyes and visualized my perfect dress. *"It's red, Lord. It has a scalloped lace neckline cut straight across, with long tight-fitting lace sleeves. It's tight at the waist, with a short skirt. I don't want to spend more than $100 for it. Thank you, Lord. **IT IS DONE!**"*

That's all I said.

I took a deep breath, dragged myself up, and headed for the last shop in the mall. I found the Formal Wear Department and made the rounds of all the racks of evening dresses. I didn't see anything even close to the dress I was looking for.

I felt disappointment settling over me; was God going to help me out or not? I'd been to every mall in a 50-mile area. If it wasn't here there was nowhere else to look.

I said, *"You've never let me down, Lord, and I know You won't let me down this time either."* I decided to go back and look through the racks again; maybe I missed something.

As I turned around to start through the racks again, a flash of red caught my eye. What was that? I turned my head and saw a saleslady walking out of the women's fitting room with a red dress in her hand — ***MY RED DRESS!***

IT HAD A SCALLOPED LACE BODICE CUT STRAIGHT ACROSS! IT HAD LONG TIGHT-FITTING LACE SLEEVES! THE TIGHT-FITTING WAIST WAS ENCIRCLED BY A BIG RED TAFFETA BOW, WITH A TAFFETA RUFFLED SHORT SKIRT FLOWING BENEATH THE BOW — EXACTLY THE DRESS I ENVISIONED IN MY MIND!

I rushed over to the saleslady and asked her if that dress was for sale. She said, *"Yes it is. We had it on hold for a lady but she never came back to claim it. I was putting it back on the rack. It's really a lovely dress, isn't it?* ***PLUS, IT'S MARKED DOWN TO ONLY $99!"***

DEAR LORD, YOU ARE SO GOOD TO ME! JUST THINK OF ALL THE TIME I WASTED TODAY RUNNING AROUND LOOKING FOR THIS DRESS WHEN I COULD HAVE ASKED YOU FIRST THING!

When I told one of my girlfriends how I got that dress, she said, *"Well, actually, Kathy, you had to end up at that mall to get the dress; it wasn't at any of the other places."* ***OH, YE OF LITTLE FAITH!***

If Jesus could take a few loaves of bread and fishes and manifest more than enough to feed 4,000 people, don't you think God could manifest this dress in the first place I looked — ***IF ONLY I HAD ASKED AT THE BEGINNING OF MY SEARCH, RATHER THAN AT THE END?***

THE MIRACLE OF MY OWN SCHOOL

After I taught the first loan processing class for the bank, the response from their employees was so positive that the bank President got the idea to offer the class to other mortgage companies. His wife was in the personnel placement business, so they both saw an opportunity for her to get to know the mortgage companies and handle their employee placement needs.

They made arrangements with Oglethorpe University to rent one of their classrooms to hold an evening class. The response from other mortgage companies was great and I taught that class for several months.

The bank ended up merging with another bank, and the new bank didn't want to continue offering the class.

I always gave the students my telephone number to call if they had questions or problem loans they needed help with, so my phone rang pretty often, and I was getting lots of phone calls from mortgage companies — since the bank wasn't going to be offering the class anymore, would I still be offering one?

I discussed it with the bank and they informed me they couldn't do it any more. They gave me their blessing — go for it! So in 1986 I created a mortgage-finance training institute. I used my favorite word that God had given me, *"capstone,"* and named my school Capstone Institute of Mortgage Finance!

I already had the format for the textbook laid out in my mind. Personally, I hadn't cared much for the materials the bank had put together for their class, so over the months that I taught their class, I created a lot of my own teaching materials — I was ready to do this!

I created the textbook and class materials, got my school incorporated, and submitted the materials to the State of Georgia Board of Education for approval as a proprietary school. All I needed now was a place to hold the classes.

Oglethorpe University couldn't provide a classroom on an ongoing basis for a daytime class, so I did a little checking around and made arrangements with Mercer University to rent a classroom on a monthly basis. I was in business!

From the very beginning my school was a big success! I was so happy with my new career, but naturally there always seems to be a problem that comes along to throw a monkey wrench into the machinery!

This was a big one and it almost shut down my school! It took another miracle to save me!

ANOTHER MIRACLE OF *"SLEEPING ON A PROBLEM AND WAKING UP WITH AN ANSWER"*

A few months after I opened the school, the news media did a big expose' on some unethical proprietary schools, such as bartending schools, pulling bums off the street to attend their school and getting them to sign up for a federally-insured student loan.

These schools weren't interested in helping people train for a new career; they were interested in collecting the student loan money. Many of these students never even attended class! Or the schools took the money and went out of business before the students could complete the courses.

The State came under a lot of pressure to make these proprietary schools more accountable for their actions, so they established a new law requiring all proprietary schools to post a $50,000 school bond.

I received notification that **I had 30 days to obtain this bond or shut down!**

When I checked into the cost of the bond, it was $5,000! Holy Cow! It might just as well have been $100,000 — I didn't have the money!

I was in a panic! I called the State and talked to the man in charge about my dilemma. While he sympathized with me, there was nothing he could do. Pay up or shut down.

I tried going to the bank to borrow the money. Although I have always maintained an impeccable credit history, my business hadn't been established long enough for the bank to take the risk. I was out of luck.

I started running around trying everything I could think of to come up with the money and worrying myself sick! I was finally down to the last week and knew if I didn't get that bond down to the State by the following Monday they would show up at my door on Tuesday to put a padlock on it!

LORDY, LORDY, WON'T I EVER LEARN? I went to bed that night feeling discouraged and depressed and said to God, *"Lord, I've done all I can. Please tell me what to do."* That's all I said before I turned out the light.

When I awoke the next morning **I HAD THE ANSWER!** What if my school were to get approved by the Real Estate Commission to teach the Real Estate Licensing Course? Wouldn't I then come under the supervision of the Real Estate Commission and not the State Board of Education? I was so excited I couldn't wait until the State office opened to call and discuss it!

The minute their office opened up I was on the phone to the man at the State. I asked him this question, *"If my school is an approved Real Estate Licensing School, would I still be required to obtain this bond or would I come under the supervision of the Real Estate Commission?"*

I heard only dead silence at the other end. Finally this man said, *"You know what, Kathy? I think that will work! Let me call you right back."*

It Is Done!

I nervously awaited his call and when it came he said, *"You were right! You can do that! If you can get approved by the Real Estate Commission before next Tuesday, I won't have to shut you down! But today is **Thursday**; do you really believe you can get it taken care of by next Tuesday?"*

I said, *"Well, I'm going to do everything in my power to make it happen! I'll be in touch!"*

Before I get into what happened next, let me digress a little. In addition to getting approved by the Georgia State Board of Education as a *"proprietary school,"* I also got my courses approved by the Georgia Real Estate Commission so Realtors could receive their required continuing education training at my school. I actually became good friends with the man at the Real Estate Commission who reviewed courses for approval. When he left to run a Real Estate Training Institute we kept in touch.

I immediately got on the phone to the woman who replaced my friend at the Real Estate Commission. I quickly swallowed my pride and just bared my soul to her about what was going on and what I needed to do; would she help me?

This woman was wonderful. She said, *"You come on down right now and I'll have the application package waiting for you out front."* I drove down, picked it up, and took it back to my office. After reviewing the information I realized I didn't know how to fill out all the paperwork, so I called my friend at the real estate school and shared my dilemma. Could he help me?

My friend told me to come on over and he would show me how to complete the paperwork. I drove over to his office, and he actually gave me a photocopy of the complete application package their school had filled out when they applied! Oh, Lord, people are so good! I rushed back to my office to fill out the paperwork.

I worked until about 11 PM that night getting the package put together. The next morning (Friday) I delivered the package to the lady at the Real Estate Commission. ***This wonderful lady took the package home with her and reviewed it over the weekend! Monday morning she called me to tell me I could pick up my approval letter!***

I rushed down to the Real Estate Commission, picked up the approval letter, and rushed over to the State Board of Education. When I handed the letter to the man I had been talking to he was stunned! He said, *"I was really hoping you could pull this off. I didn't want to shut you down, but I didn't see any way that you could possibly accomplish this in three days! This is a miracle!"*

I smiled and said, *"Yes, that's exactly what it is — a miracle!"* As I drove back to my office, I reviewed the events of the last few days and shook my head.

I said, *"You know, Lord, when will I learn to **ASK YOU FIRST?** If I had done that when this problem first came up, it would have been resolved weeks ago! Please help me remember this lesson."*

I didn't even have a chance to take a deep breath and relax before I was hit with another crisis! Once again, a miracle saved me!

It Is Done!

THE MIRACLE OF CLASSROOM SPACE

Mercer University informed me that they wouldn't be able to provide a classroom anymore! Now what was I going to do?

I flew into a panic! I already had a class scheduled at that location next month! I had to find another place to hold classes right away! What was I going to tell my students? Where was I going to go?

After the horrifying experience I'd just been through, I was both physically and emotionally exhausted and in no frame of mind to deal with another crisis so quickly. This time, I decided to ***ASK GOD FOR HELP UP FRONT, NOT AFTER I'D EXHAUSTED ALL MY OWN RESOURCES,*** so I asked God to find the perfect place for me to hold my classes. I was too tired to worry about it.

The quicker we can release the issue to God — ***AND LEAVE IT WITH GOD*** — the quicker things will happen. I believe my answer came so quickly because I just totally and completely released it! I didn't have long to wait!

HERE'S ANOTHER MIRACLE! That same week I received a phone call from a gentleman in the mortgage business who was currently taking a class at the Investment Training Institute to get his securities license. While he was attending the class, the owner of the school mentioned to the group that he had some vacant classrooms he was interested in renting out; if they knew of anyone who might be interested, have them give him a call

— AND THIS MAN THOUGHT OF ME! THANK YOU, LORD!

I scheduled a meeting with the owner and ended up renting a classroom from this wonderful man for *three years! I NEVER EVEN HAD TO GO OUT AND SEARCH FOR A CLASSROOM!*

THIS IS HOW EASY IT REALLY IS — YOU ASK, GOD PROVIDES!

IT WAS TIME TO MAKE SOME CHANGES

The five years I spent with my husband were not happy years. During those years I was in the only automobile accident I've been in to date, and it left me with a permanent pain in the upper right side of my back. I also developed a severe case of arthritis in my fingers.

The arthritis got so bad that I couldn't even hold the steering wheel to drive, nor could I type anymore. Something had to be done — this was interfering with my business! Taking drugs to ease the pain wasn't for me, because it didn't cure the problem! There had to be a better way!

This arthritis had to stop! My sister, who was going through chemotherapy for cancer at that time, gave me a rubber ball her doctor had given her to squeeze to strengthen her hands.

I began squeezing that rubber ball all day long, first one hand, then the other. And every time my fingers started hurting I'd say *"Thank You, Lord, for taking away the pain — there is no pain."*

I absolutely refused to give in to this thing! I couldn't let it interfere with my business. I am the most driven human being in the world!

Gradually, with the squeezing of the rubber ball and my refusal to acknowledge the pain, it went away. I've had no problems since that time.

Years later I read the wonderful book by Louise Hay, *"You Can Heal Your Life,"* which discusses the emotional causes of physical illness, and how we can literally cure ourselves of any illness. I flipped to the back of the book and looked at the list of problems and probable causes.

Here is what it said about arthritic fingers: *"A desire to punish. Blame. Feeling victimized."*

OH BROTHER! DID THAT EVER DESCRIBE ME AT THAT TIME IN MY LIFE!

There I was in a very unhappy marriage, feeling victimized and unloved, blaming myself for getting into that terrible situation. Could I create a case of arthritic fingers? Apparently I did!

While I was pleased that my school was doing so well, there were many sad events taking place. I watched helplessly as my sister lost her battle with cancer and my Mother lost her battle with emphysema, dying within two months of each other. My Dad was completely lost after my Mother died, especially after he retired and had nothing to fill his days.

My husband was very kind and supportive of me during those difficult days. While I appreciated his kindness, we both realized that we just weren't compatible and mutually agreed to a divorce.

We agreed that he would get 100% ownership in the building company and I would get 100% ownership in my school, and I talked to my Dad about moving in with him.

It Is Done!

He liked the idea and certainly had lots of room, so in the fall of 1988 I packed up my stuff and moved in with him.

I've looked back over the years I lived with my Dad, and it seems that those were my real "learning" years. It started when I was moving a box of books into my new bedroom and one of the books fell out and hit me on my foot.

I picked it up and looked at the title, *"Edgar Cayce, The Sleeping Prophet,"* by Jess Stern. Hmmm...I bought that book way back in the '70s and never read it; maybe it was time.

Once I got settled in I began reading this book. It told the story of the remarkable psychic and healer, Edgar Cayce. Cayce had the ability to go into a sleep trance, during which time his wife or secretary would ask him to diagnose a particular ailment for a person.

Cayce would correctly diagnose the ailment and prescribe a treatment. He was pretty much one hundred percent accurate in his diagnoses and treatments, and soon people were coming from all over the country to receive help.

I read with interest that on one occasion while in trance Cayce diagnosed the ailment and treatment for a particular person and ended his trance by saying something to the effect that, *"The entity (the man for whom he was giving a reading) was a monk in a former lifetime."*

When he came out of his trance and his wife and secretary related what he had said, it upset him greatly.

Cayce had strong faith, read the entire Bible every year of his life, and believed that the concept of former lifetimes — reincarnation — was not in keeping with Christian teachings. It created a real dilemma for him.

He sincerely felt that he was able to help people while in his trance state, but he didn't know about this reincarnation issue; he needed to do some serious praying and soul searching. He couldn't continue his readings if he didn't feel the information he was providing to these people was from God.

Cayce came to the conclusion that reincarnation was very much in keeping with his belief in life after death. His research turned up the fact that many parts of the original Bible text did discuss reincarnation, but in the Fourth Century when Constantine convened a council of religious leaders in Rome to put the Bible into a written text, the Council of Nicaea, as they were called, made the decision to remove all mention of reincarnation on the pretext that *"the ignorant masses wouldn't understand."* (I think it was more a matter of *"Let's tell the ignorant masses that they only have one shot in this lifetime at being 'saved,' and their only salvation is to come to us."*)

At any rate, Cayce continued his readings for many people, but now included past-life readings as well. He found that many ailments suffered today were created by an incident that occurred in a previous lifetime. For example, a man who experienced panic attacks where he felt he was choking and couldn't breathe discovered that he had been hanged in a former lifetime.

It Is Done!

Cayce was able to relieve the suffering of many people for whom mainstream medical treatments failed, simply by describing the traumatic experience from the former lifetime and allowing the person to "release" it.

It was a fascinating book and opened up a whole new world for me! It started my odyssey to find out as much as I could about reincarnation. Asking for God's guidance, I began visiting bookstores. Once, while I was turning a bookstand around and reading book titles, a book fell on my foot — for the second time! It was entitled *"A World Beyond,"* by Ruth Montgomery. I read the entire book in a couple of hours — then rushed back to the bookstore to purchase all of her other books!

Because of my Christian background, the concept of reincarnation made me feel uneasy, just as it had Edgar Cayce, but these books made so much sense! I gave them to my Dad and asked him to read them and give me his opinion, which I greatly respected. My Dad came to the same conclusion — they made sense to him! We had many wonderful discussions on the topic.

That was a good year for me. My life was calm, I was reading lots of spiritual books and learning some wonderful truths, and my Dad and I got re-acquainted.

My school was doing well, so when one of my girlfriends told me I should check into leasing some office space in the same building where her office was located, I checked into it.

She was actually sub-leasing space from another tenant and told me there was plenty of room for me as well. I could sub-lease my office from the current tenants without having to sign a long-term lease and just sign a lease with the landlord for enough space to conduct the classes. That way, I wouldn't be biting off more than I could chew.

I was moving up in the world!

It Is Done!

THE MIRACLE OF MY CLASSROOM DESKS AND CHAIRS

I signed a five-year lease for about 1,500 square feet for my classroom and sub-leased some office space where my girlfriend's office was located, sharing a Receptionist and copier room with the other people in the office. Now I had another problem — where in the world would I get the desks and chairs needed for the classroom?

I checked into purchasing from an office supply store and almost had a heart attack! The type of desks I needed for the classroom would cost about $150 each and the chairs would cost $45 each! If I wanted 100 desks at $150 each, that was $15,000, and 100 chairs at $45 each was another $4,500 — ***THAT WAS A TOTAL OF $19,500! I CERTAINLY DID NOT HAVE THAT KIND OF MONEY!***

So I took it to God! I told God that I needed 100 desks and chairs for my classroom; would He please find them for me? Then I picked up the yellow pages of the telephone book and started calling used office furniture stores. I explained my needs to each of these stores, asking them to keep their eyes open.

In one day I called about five different places, with no luck, but I wasn't giving up! God always came through for me! And of course He did this time also! When I called yet another used office furniture store and described what I was looking for, I heard only silence from the man at the other end. I wondered what was going on.

He said, *"It's funny you should be calling me. I don't usually purchase classroom desks and chairs but just last week I had an opportunity to buy all of the office furniture from a school in Louisiana. I didn't really want the desks and chairs, but I had to take the whole lot — **I'LL SELL YOU THE DESKS FOR $15 EACH AND THE CHAIRS FOR $10 EACH.**"*

I WAS THRILLED! 100 DESKS AT $15.00 EACH CAME TO $1,500, AND 100 CHAIRS AT $10.00 EACH CAME TO $1,000! I HAD FURNISHED MY ENTIRE CLASSROOM FOR $2,500 — <u>NOT</u> $19,500! THANK YOU, LORD!

It Is Done!

THE MIRACLE OF THE LOST EMERALD

I was feeling so good about everything! I had a new classroom, I had new tables and chairs for the classroom, the classes were filling up and I was on top of the world! After one particularly hectic day of running to about five different places before making it to the office, I walked into my office and laid my briefcase on my desk. As I looked down to open the briefcase I gasped in shock — the emerald in my ring was missing!

This particular emerald ring was given to me by my grandmother and was one of my favorites! Where in the world did I lose the stone, and why did it have to be that particular day, when I'd been all over kingdom come? I'd never find that stone!

When I got beyond my panic attack I took a deep breath and said a prayer, *"Lord, this ring means quite a lot to me and I know that emerald is here for me to find. I thank You for helping me find it.* ***IT IS DONE!"*** I then began the search for the lost emerald, walking slowly through the building, out through the parking lot, and all around my car.

Nope, it wasn't there. I got into my car and began retracing my steps to the places I had been to that day. I didn't see it at the second place so I drove to the third place. I parked in the same space as before and started walking slowly around the parking lot, moving toward the office building.

All of a sudden it felt like two hands literally took hold of my face and forced it to look down in a certain direction — *AND THERE WAS MY EMERALD!* I was so overjoyed that I had found it that I sang praises to God all the way back to my office! ***Thank You, Lord! You are so good to me!***

ILLNESS STRIKES — FOLLOWED BY A MIRACULOUS HEALING

During the time I was running around getting my office and classroom set up, I began to experience excessive fatigue. I found that after teaching a class it was all I could do to make it home and to bed. The fatigue persisted, followed by problems with digesting anything I ate. I lost my appetite completely and began losing weight at an alarming rate.

When I finally consulted a physician I was shocked to discover that I had contracted Hepatitis B, for which there was really no treatment. The doctor instructed me to get "plenty of bed rest." My research turned up the scary fact that a substantial number of people died from this disease!

This was a very frightening and frustrating time for me, as I was unable to teach and had to postpone my classes. Unfortunately, monthly business-related bills still had to be paid, so I was forced to draw from my charge cards (at exorbitant interest rates) to keep the bills paid.

I was forced to stay at home, languishing in bed, with nothing to do but worry about the future of my school. I was so blessed to have my Dad there to take care of me, but it frustrated me that I wasn't getting any better.

I knew I was in serious trouble when my skin and eyeballs turned yellow — a sign of yellow jaundice and subsequent liver failure. I didn't even have the strength to pray, but fortunately God was there watching out for me.

One Sunday, about four weeks into my illness, I received a phone call from a former student, Ava Lee, asking how I was feeling. She told me later that something in my voice alarmed her so she asked if she could stop by to see me. Not wanting her to 'catch' my hepatitis I tried to dissuade her, but she was adamant.

Ava showed up at my Dad's home, took one look at me, and said, *"You are very sick, Kathy. You're coming with me to see my doctor."* In spite of my protests she practically shoved me out the door into her car and drove me to an oriental doctor she knew. The doctor tried to take my blood pressure and couldn't get a reading. Then she tried to read my pulse but couldn't find that either! I quipped, *"Does this mean I'm dead?"*

This doctor looked at me and said, *"This is not funny; you are very sick!"* She then started pulling herbs out of jars and putting together a mixture for me to brew and drink. I had to use a special earthenware pot to brew this concoction and I knew from the way it smelled that it would taste even worse, but she was adamant about taking it immediately.

The total cost of this visit was $35.00, including the herbs! No wonder mainstream medical doctors refuse to accept alternative treatments — there's not enough money in it to pay for their country clubs and golf carts! At any rate, I took these herbs home and brewed them in my special earthenware pot, poured the brew into a cup, added some honey to kill the taste, held my nose, and drank it. Ughhh! It tasted horrible, but a few hours later I found that I was hungry and enjoyed a meal for the first time in weeks!

It Is Done!

I drank that vile brew for only three days and was back up on my feet! What a miracle that Ava was guided to call and visit me, and what a miracle that only an oriental doctor could provide the cure I needed. ***Thank You, Lord!***

I was able to go back to work the following week and jumped in headfirst, trying to catch up on the lost income by scheduling way too many classes through the week, in the evening, and on the weekends.

Needless to say, I overdid it and ended up collapsing from exhaustion.

When my chest started hurting, I thought I was having a heart attack but it turned out to be pneumonia! I had no idea pneumonia could be so painful! I couldn't take a breath without feeling a piercing pain in my chest. Once again, I was flat on my back and unable to sleep at night because of the pain and difficulty in breathing. Once again, my wonderful Dad took care of me or I would have ended up in the hospital.

One morning about 6 AM I was wide-awake, unable to sleep because of the pain and difficulty in breathing when I heard the doorbell ring downstairs. My Dad got out of bed and went to the door and I heard a man's voice talking to him. The next thing I knew, my Dad was coming up the stairs to my bedroom followed by a policeman. What in the world was going on here?

This poor man felt so bad about what he had to do when he saw how sick I was, but he was just doing his job — he had to deliver a Summons to me from a local lumber company who was suing me for $50,000 worth of building materials purchased from their warehouse but never paid for.

When I divorced and gave my ex-husband ownership of my building company, I wrote letters to all creditors advising them of the ownership change and that I would no longer be liable for debts incurred by the building company. Unfortunately I missed one.

This building materials company was one I had set up a line of credit with but never used. I forgot about them but evidently my ex-husband didn't! Not being able to obtain credit in his own name due to his bad credit history, he found this unused account still open and proceeded to charge up the credit line and not pay the bills!

Oh Lord, what else was going to happen? I was too sick to even do anything about it at that point; all I could do was lie there feeling angry and helpless. Two years after our divorce, my ex-husband had run the building company into the ground; he built homes that didn't sell (which was very hard for me to believe since the housing market was excellent at that time) and defaulted on his construction loans and supplier debts. He then skipped town and fled back to his parents in Florida. Coward!

When I got back up on my feet, I had to pay for the services of a lawyer to work out the details, which dragged on and on.

In the meantime I was struggling to get my teaching schedule back on track and dealing with about $35,000 in credit card debt I had charged up to keep the school going while I was sick.

It Is Done!

I was so overwhelmed by this mountain of debt that it was hard for me to function, especially since I've tried to live my life debt-free. How in the world would I ever pay off this debt when new bills were coming in every day?

I finally made the decision to pay off the entire debt in one year! I decided to take each bill and divide the balance by 52 weeks, then make payments every week. Weekly payments I could stomach, but I just couldn't bring myself to write a huge check each month for each bill!

I told God, *"Lord, I know You don't want me to be in debt and I know the money is here to make these payments, and I thank You for bringing the students to me to make these weekly payments. Thank You, Lord!* ***IT IS DONE!"***

AND AGAIN, GOD DID PROVIDE! Every week enough money came in to make those payments and I was able to pay the entire amount within 12 months! I was debt-free again!

IT WAS TIME FOR SOME PROFESSIONAL HELP

This time in my life was stressful to say the least! I really didn't give myself time to fully recuperate from my illnesses before I threw myself back into teaching, writing, and running the school. I knew I was in serious trouble when I called a friend one night and got his answering machine asking me to leave my name and telephone number. Problem was, I couldn't remember my home telephone number! I panicked and had to go downstairs to ask my Dad what my home telephone number was!

As if that weren't bad enough, one day at work I ran into the same problem when I called a business associate and got an answering machine asking me to leave my name and telephone number. I couldn't remember my business phone number either! I had to scramble around and find a business card with my number on it!

After I left a message and hung up the phone I began thinking about this experience and realized I was in serious trouble and needed some help.

I thought about my options, which were to go to a psychiatrist (that would take way too long and cost way too much money) or I could go to a counselor at church (which didn't really appeal to me either). What to do?

I closed my eyes and said, *"Lord, I'm in serious trouble here and I need some help. Will You please guide me to the right person? I know that person is out there!"* Almost immediately I remembered a former student from

It Is Done!

over a year ago who told me about a man who helped her work through some of her problems, and remembered she had given me this man's business card...what did I do with that card? I began shuffling through the papers and business cards in my desk drawer and found his card — Rev. Dr. Jack Bernard Moon.

It turned out that this man (who worked out of his apartment) was right down the street from me! I decided to call him and schedule an appointment.

This very kind gentleman told me later that when I walked into his apartment he saw a woman who was literally on her last leg, and he saw no one around me who could help me — I was on my own!

He had me lie down on a table and led me into a relaxed, calm state and while he worked on my energies I proceeded to have very clear visions!

In my first session I very clearly saw myself sitting on a bench in a garden — looking into the beautiful face of Jesus — yes, Jesus!

Jesus smiled at me and said, *"Kathy, I want you to forgive — (my ex-husband)."*

My response was, *"Lord, I have forgiven him."*

Jesus smiled again and said, *"No, Kathy, you haven't."*

I responded, *"Well, look what he's done to me — it isn't fair!"*

"I'll take care of your problem," he said gently. *"You must forgive him."*

I cried, *"But Lord, it's $50,000!"*

Unfazed by my comment, he said, *"I told you I'll take care of it."*

How could I respond; it was pretty clear, wasn't it? I promised him I would work very hard on forgiveness. I sensed my lack thereof was creating some of the physical illnesses, stress, and forgetfulness in my life.

My therapist assured me that I wasn't hallucinating; I really **"saw what I saw,"** and was quite surprised that I was able to get such a vivid image so quickly, which told both of us that I was on the right track.

I had four sessions altogether and with each session my images were vivid and very real, mostly dealing with feelings of guilt about the deaths of my mother and sister and my feelings of helplessness in not being able to do more to help them.

I also saw my tendency to fall into very negative "poor me" pity-party moods and recognized how this negative thought process was holding me back from accomplishing all that I desired to accomplish. It was a life-changing experience!

During my last session once again I had a most vivid experience where I saw myself walking down a path. As I came around a curve in the path I observed a huge bull to the side of the path with his head down and horns pointed

It Is Done!

directly at me, snorting and pawing the ground, ready to charge me.

Rather than being frightened I calmly walked over to the bull and placed my hand on his head, at which point he immediately calmed down, became very docile, and began grazing in the grass.

I continued to walk down the path and as I came around another corner I saw many people who appeared to be quite desperate, frantically looking around for something or someone. Their clothing was torn and dirty and they seemed quite upset.

As soon as they saw me, they all came running toward me and began clawing at my clothing; one man fell on the ground and wrapped his arms around my legs!

Once again, rather than being frightened, I just calmly released all of them in a gentle manner and continued walking down the path, but I turned around to see what these people were doing. It appeared they had already forgotten me and were once again frantically searching for someone else to grab on to!

As I continued down the path around another curve I observed a court jester, the image we see on a deck of playing cards, laughing, pointing his finger, and shaking his wand as if to mock or make fun of me. I calmly walked over to him and placed my hand gently on his shoulder and he slumped down, turned away, and skulked off.

I continued down the path and came around another curve and was stunned to see hundreds of people waiting for me!

These people all appeared to be well dressed, intelligent and well educated and when they saw me they began clapping their hands as they rushed forward, picked me up and began carrying me, cheering all the way!

I was stunned by this vision! What in the world did it mean? I described what I had seen to my therapist and asked him what it meant. He said, *"Whoa, lady, that's a pretty powerful vision! Give me a minute to digest this and ask for guidance."*

He sat quietly for a moment with his eyes closed, meditating on what I had described to him and then said, *"The bull you saw, pawing the ground ready to charge you, represents the financial problems you've been experiencing lately in your life. The ease with which you walked over and calmed the bull indicates the ease with which you will overcome these financial problems. In other words, don't worry about it, it's all going to work out very smoothly.*

"The people you saw pulling at you represent the people in your life who are 'users,' obviously a problem you've had for a long time!

"You gently released them and kept walking — BUT because you felt guilty you turned around to look back and witnessed what you already knew was the truth — if you don't help them they will just keep looking for someone else to hang on to! This is a lesson you needed to learn.

*"The court jester represents **YOU** constantly putting*

your-self down and beating yourself up for 'not being good enough.' Once again, your gentle handling of this situation indicates this lesson is one that you will be overcoming.

*"The final vision, with the people cheering for you and carrying you represents your **DESTINY**. There will come a time in your life when you will be able to share your experiences and the way you've been able to overcome adversity and fear, and you will help these people as well overcome their own adversity and fears."*

When he finished speaking I sat there stunned, totally overwhelmed and unable to speak. My spirit told me that he spoke the truth and something deep inside of me confirmed what I had known all along — I am a teacher with a sincere desire to help people understand, not only about mortgage financing but also about the wonderful life they can live if they learn to trust that God will take care of them.

I realized that I had been doing some of this in my classes when I mentioned God and shared some of the wonderful miracles that I had experienced. I knew from some of the nice letters I received from former students that the spiritual part of my classes did help them in ways I never dreamed of.

Although I sometimes wondered if I should "cool it with the religious stuff" in my classes I was totally powerless to do that, since God had always been such a permanent part of my life. It was impossible for me to talk to anyone without mentioning God. In a way I felt this was my confirmation that it was "OK" to talk about God to anybody and everybody I came in contact with.

This experience has stayed with me now for 12 years, and I still see my vision just as vividly as I saw it all those many years ago.

My sessions with Jack Moon left me with much to think about. I guess the most comforting part was that I trusted that my many financial problems would be resolved, especially relating to the $50,000 lawsuit my ex-husband had stuck me with. I hadn't heard anything from the attorneys in some time and I guess I believed *"no news was good news."*

This experience also gave me an insatiable desire to learn as much about spiritual things as I could, so I began spending many hours at the bookstore browsing through the shelves. Once again a book literally fell on my feet and when I bent down to pick it up I heard a voice say *"Read this book!"* The title of the book was *"The Power of Your Subconscious Mind"* by Dr. Joseph Murphy.

This is one book that I still read to this day, over and over again. This was my first experience with the concept of training your subconscious mind to attract health and wealth into your life.

The concept of *"positive affirmations"* also interested me and I began practicing them all the time.

It was so thrilling to learn that I could *"affirm"* anything in my life that I wanted, from something as small as the best parking place to more business to...well, just about anything I wanted. I felt totally alive again and was so excited about my spiritual journey!

It Is Done!

THIS STUFF REALLY WORKS! When I first started getting into *"Positive Thinking,"* I tried it once when I was looking for a parking space. Naturally when I first pulled in to the parking lot my old *"negative thinking"* kicked in and I thought, *"I'm never going to find a decent parking space!"*

After driving around and around looking for a parking space, getting more and more frustrated, I finally just stopped my car, put my hands on the steering wheel and said out loud, *"I affirm a parking space is here just waiting for me RIGHT NOW! Thank You, Lord!"*

I took a deep breath, started moving forward — and ***ALMOST RAN INTO A CAR THAT WAS PULLING OUT OF A PARKING SPACE! I couldn't believe it! IT WORKED!*** So I immediately pulled into the space. As I got out of my car and walked toward the store, I started thinking, *"Yeah, I got a parking space, but it's half a mile from the store!"* ***THERE'S MY OLD "NEGATIVE THINKING" AGAIN!***

When I realized what I was doing, I stopped and started laughing! I said, *"I take that back! I'm just grateful, God, that I got a space at all! And the next time I'll affirm a space **RIGHT UP FRONT!***"

AND THAT'S WHAT I STARTED DOING! Since then, every time I need to park in a big lot I affirm a parking space up front from the moment I pull into the lot — ***AND IT ALWAYS WORKS!***

Once I had to run to the mall one day before Christmas, and traffic was bumper to bumper getting into the parking lot. So I began chanting, while I crawled along, *"Thank you, God, for the perfect parking space...Thank you, God, for the perfect parking space...."* Just as I pulled into the covered parking garage — *A CAR PULLED OUT — THE PERFECT PARKING SPACE!*

Once when my sister-in-law and I went shopping together, she pulled into the parking lot at the mall, which was packed, and immediately said, *"Oh my gosh! Would you look at this full lot! We'll NEVER find a parking space!"*

I just smiled at her and told her to repeat after me, *"Thank you, God, for the PERFECT PARKING SPACE RIGHT UP FRONT! Thank you, God, for the PERFECT PARKING SPACE RIGHT UP FRONT!"* She just stared at me like I was some kind of nut! I said, *"Come on! Do it! It works every time for me!"* She shrugged her shoulders and said, *"OK, you weirdo! If you say so!"*

So we both proceeded down the lot, chanting our little words, with me directing her to the FRONT OF THE LOT — *SURE ENOUGH, A CAR PULLED OUT PRACTICALLY IN THE FIRST PARKING SPACE NEXT TO THE MALL!*

My sister-in-law whipped into the space, turned to me and said, *"What are you, some kind of witch or something?"* I just laughed and said, *"Nope, I'm only affirming God's promise that He will give me the DESIRES OF MY HEART — NO MATTER HOW SMALL THEY MAY SEEM!"*

It Is Done!

A few months later my sister-in-law told me that she and a friend of hers entered the parking lot at the mall and ran into the same situation — the lot was packed. Her friend started moaning, *"Will you look at this place! It's packed! We'll never get a parking space!"*

My sister-in-law looked at her and said, *"Well, my sister-in-law Kathy says all we have to do is affirm the perfect parking space and we'll get it! It won't hurt to try! Let's go, repeat after me..."* So they began to repeat my little chant while my sister-in-law headed toward the front of the lot — ***AND SURE ENOUGH A CAR PULLED OUT OF THE "PERFECT SPOT" AND SHE PULLED IN!***

She and her friend had a really good laugh over this! So now her friend does the old ***AFFIRMING THE PERFECT PARKING SPACE*** every time she goes out, and she's passed it along to her friends...***AND SO IT GOES! TRY IT, THEN PASS IT ALONG TO YOUR FRIENDS!***

SEE HOW POWERFUL YOUR THOUGHTS AND WORDS ARE? LEARN TO TURN YOUR "NEGATIVE THOUGHT PATTERNS" TO "POSITIVE THOUGHT PATTERNS!"

When my father became very ill and had to be hospitalized, each evening after work I would drive to the hospital to see him. Since I resented having to pay for parking in the covered parking lot, I always *"affirmed"* a free parking space on the "U-shaped" driveway that looped up to the front door of the hospital and back down the other side. I always got one, too!

One particular evening, while I was driving to the hospital, I was absolutely exhausted from a hard day of standing on my feet teaching all day.

I kept thinking that I always got a parking space somewhere around that "U-shaped" driveway, but it was usually pretty far away, and then I had to trudge up the hill to the hospital. I didn't think I could do it that night, I was so tired.

So this time, while I was driving to the hospital I kept repeating, *"I affirm a parking space **RIGHT AT THE FRONT DOOR!**"* As I pulled into the driveway of the hospital, I didn't see a single parking space anywhere on the driveway! But I wasn't going to get discouraged.

As I came up the driveway toward the front of the hospital I kept repeating, *"I affirm a parking space **RIGHT AT THE FRONT DOOR!**"* Just as I came up to the front door — ***A CAR PULLED OUT OF A PARKING SPACE <u>RIGHT AT THE FRONT DOOR</u>!*** Believe me, I grabbed that space immediately, all the time thanking God for honoring my request!

ANOTHER MIRACLE ANSWERED BY *"SLEEPING ON IT"*

The sessions that I went through with Jack Moon helped me tremendously and I felt I was back on track. My peace of mind, however, was short-lived! I got a phone call from the landlord, who said, *"We hate to tell you this, Kathy. The tenants you're sub-leasing your offices from haven't paid the rent in months — we're evicting all of you."*

Oh great! Another crisis! We all paid the tenants to sub-lease office space and they pocketed the money and didn't pay their rent! What was I going to do? I couldn't move my office into the classroom! I was paying for my office plus a proportionate share of the rent for the Receptionist and copier area. I would be forced to rent enough space to accommodate my needs. In addition, I now needed a Receptionist full time!

When things like this happened, I always flew into a tizzy and fell into the old *"pity party"* pattern: *"Why do these things keep happening? Why can't things just run smoothly? Why must there always be crises to deal with..."* and on and on.

Then, I would stop and think, *"Well, maybe this is another opportunity for God to show me how well He takes care of me!"* After spending about a week moaning, groaning, and wondering how I was going to handle new office space ***plus*** the salary of a Receptionist, I finally decided to sleep on it. I *"affirmed"* the perfect situation that included an office space big enough to accommodate both my administrative needs as well as my classroom needs, and I thanked God for taking care of it for me.

After I finished teaching class the next day, I ran into a man who also had office space in the building. His office was located next to the classroom so we got to know each other pretty well as I came and went to class. He told me he heard about what happened and asked me to follow him.

He took me around to the other side of the building and opened the door to one of the offices. I looked around and couldn't believe my eyes! It was a room large enough to accommodate my class! I followed him through the other offices in the space and saw a Receptionist area and two other large offices. Altogether, the space comprised about 2,000 square feet. It was perfect for me!

He told me the tenants had just moved out that week and he knew the space was available. Why didn't I talk to the landlord about re-negotiating my lease for that space? Since I was increasing my square footage from 1,500 to 2,000 they would probably go for it.

And that's what I did! I called the landlord and asked to move to the other space. They readily agreed and we negotiated a new lease for the larger space. As for the extra monthly expenses I was incurring, I just trusted that God would provide.

I now needed to hire a Receptionist, so I *"affirmed"* the perfect person and thanked God for finding someone for me. Sure enough, He provided someone immediately.

It Is Done!

I mentioned to the students in my class that I would be moving my classroom to a space around the corner and would be looking for a Receptionist. After class, one of my students came over to me and told me that his sister was looking for a job and he would have her give me a call.

I liked his sister very much and hired her on the spot! Her salary requirements were within the range I had in mind, so she came to work right away and helped me get my new office set up and organized. ***WHY CAN'T I LEARN THAT THIS IS HOW EASILY ALL PROBLEMS CAN BE HANDLED?***

THE MIRACLE OF THE FREE FAX MACHINE

Once I got my new office set up and organized, I started thinking about purchasing a fax machine. Fax machines were just becoming popular at that time and I saw it as a way to save money.

If I could fax out a flyer advertising my classes rather than sending out a monthly mailing, it would reduce expenses. Money was a little tight since I had to pay for a new phone system, movers, and my new Receptionist's salary. I decided to *"affirm"* my new fax machine and thanked God for getting it for me.

Sure enough, it wasn't a week later that I received a phone call from a former student. This man had taken my class over a year ago and had never paid for the class.

I knew at the time he came in to talk to me about taking the class that he was having some financial problems, so I allowed him to take the class with the promise that he would pay me later.

I had completely forgotten about this man! If there is one thing I had learned over the years in my growing relationship with God, it was to forgive debts. If they paid, so be it, and if they didn't, let it go.

The truth is, when people don't pay the debts, it's because they **FEAR** there won't be enough money to go around. Since *"thoughts are things,"* that's what they get — not enough money to go around. Paying your debts and

It Is Done!

trusting that the money will come in opens the channel to receive the money — from whatever source! Don't worry about where it's coming from! Just accept that it's coming!

This man was calling me because he knew he still owed me for the class, but he was wondering — ***WOULD I ACCEPT A BRAND NEW FAX MACHINE AS PAYMENT FOR HIS DEBT?***

Somebody traded the fax machine to him for something else but he didn't need it. It was still in the box!

I used that fax machine up until a couple of years ago! It served me well!

THE JOY OF
"POSITIVE AFFIRMATIONS"

This was a very good time for me. I was reading more and more about spiritual principles that were available to everyone, if we would just *"seek and ye shall find."* I especially enjoyed the positive affirmations and found myself *"affirming"* everything from students signing up for my classes to the perfect dress, parking place...you name it, I affirmed it!

I especially liked my discovery about the perfect parking space. I told everyone about my new discovery only to be chastised for *"taking advantage of God's good graces,"* as one friend put it. I was totally bewildered by this reaction until I started remembering how I also had felt that way at one time.

I discovered that most people didn't feel they should be asking God for such mundane things as a parking space. They felt that one should only call upon God in an emergency, when all other avenues have been exhausted.

I thought back over the past few years about the wonderful things that God had done for me and I wondered if I was asking too much. Was it really frivolous to ask for such mundane things?

I re-read some of the books that had made such an impact on my life and came to the realization that what these books were saying was that ***God has already provided everything we need in this life*** and the act of *"affirming"* our desires was the same as saying *"Thank You, God, for providing."* It was really that simple.

The issue was to *"be ye as children."* Children ask their father or mother for everything, totally accepting that their needs will be provided for. God also wanted us to *"ask our Father"* for whatever our desires were and He would always *"give us the desires of our heart."*

Why don't churches teach this? Why must they fill us with the fear of God and not allow the love of God to enter our hearts? I know how many years I spent fearing God, feeling unworthy of anything until I came to the realization that God never expected me to be perfect.

I was talking to a friend, who lived in Kansas at that time, about my new discoveries and she moaned, *"Well, I wish it would work for me! I really need to find a job, but I don't want to work full-time since I want to be here when Stephanie gets home from school. About the only job I've been able to find is working at WalMart, and that just doesn't appeal to me."*

I decided it was time to get her on the right path. I asked, *"What is your image of the perfect job?"*

She said, *"Well, gee, I don't have any idea!"*

I said, *"Yes you do! If you could do anything you wanted, what would you do?"*

She thought about it for awhile and said, *"What I'd really like to do is teach computer courses. I've really been getting into them lately. Of course, there's no way I could possibly teach computer courses! I'm sure they're looking for someone with a Masters Degree in Computer Science!"*

My response was, *"Well, you won't know unless you try. Let's try something. Let's imagine the perfect situation. What is your perfect situation?"*

She said, *"Well, I really don't know."*

I said, *"YES YOU DO! NOW TELL ME WHAT THE PERFECT SITUATION IS!"*

She finally sighed and said, *"Well, I guess the perfect situation is working at a job I really like, such as teaching computer courses."*

I said, *"What else?"*

"What do you mean, what else? Isn't that enough?" she asked.

I said, *"If you want to get exactly what you want, you must AFFIRM exactly what you want. Didn't you mention that you wanted to be home each day when Stephanie got home from school? What about the location? Is there a perfect distance you have to drive? What about your salary? Is there a perfect salary you want to make? You see what I'm getting at? You must be SPECIFIC about what you want! Now tell me what you want!"*

She said, *"Well, I guess I'd like to work somewhere that won't take more than fifteen or twenty minutes to get there, and I do want to be here when Stephanie gets home*

It Is Done!

from school," she said. *"I guess maybe $ —— is what I had in mind for my salary."*

I said, *"OK, here we go. Repeat after me: 'I affirm the perfect job is here RIGHT NOW! I am teaching computer courses. I drive no more than fifteen to twenty minutes to work. I'm home each day when Stephanie comes home from school, and my salary is $ ——. IT IS DONE!'"*

After we completed our affirmation, I said, *"Now go get the yellow pages and look up computer schools. DO IT RIGHT NOW!"*

She put the phone down and got the telephone book. *"OK, I'm looking in the telephone book under computer schools. It looks like there are quite a few of them! What should I do now?"*

I said, *"Look for the ones that are within fifteen to twenty minutes of your house, pick up the phone and tell them you're looking for a computer training job! All they can do to you is say 'NO!' What do you have to lose? I want you to call some schools and call me back when you get one that's interested in talking to you."*

"Yeah, sure," she said. *"They'll be thrilled to talk to me, I'm sure."*

I sighed, *"Well, with that attitude you won't get anything! Don't you understand that you have to TRULY BELIEVE IT'S POSSIBLE IN ORDER TO MAKE IT HAPPEN? Don't you know that 'THOUGHTS ARE THINGS?' Whatever you think is what you get! I guarantee it will work! Now get to it and call me back!"*

After I hung up the phone I had my doubts that she would be successful, especially since I knew how important it was to not only **SPEAK** the words but to **BELIEVE WHAT YOU WERE SPEAKING!** Did my friend really believe strongly enough? I said my own silent prayer to God asking Him to help her; then I sat back and waited for her call.

She called me back within the hour to tell me, *"I can't believe this! I only had to call two schools and it turns out that the second school I called is looking for computer teachers! I've got an appointment tomorrow to meet with them! I just can't believe this!"*

She got the job! She began her computer-training career, she was home when her daughter got home from school, she drove only fifteen minutes to the school and they paid her what she wanted! ***ISN'T GOD GREAT!***

THE MIRACLE OF MY NEW CAR

Affirming everything became a way of life for me. I looked forward to getting up each day and anticipating the wonderful things God was doing in my life. This even extended to the perfect car!

A friend of mine asked me to keep her car while she went on assignment for six months in Europe. It was a Bonneville SSEI. While she was gone, I fell in love with that car and when she came back to reclaim it, I was devastated!

I wanted one! So I went to a dealership and bought one! I completed an application for the car loan and received a phone call the next day telling me I was approved. I just needed to come back in, sign the paperwork, and the car was mine.

Then I started thinking about what I had done. I just bought a car that cost ***$32,000! THAT'S HOW MUCH I SPENT FOR MY FIRST HOUSE YEARS AGO!*** Did I really want to do this? Why didn't I get a used one instead?

When I called the dealership and told them I decided to get a Bonneville SSEI that was one year old, the salesman laughed at me! He told me that I would never find it. The car was pretty popular and a one-year-old model just wasn't available.

Naturally, I didn't believe him. Well, I called every dealer in Atlanta, including a dealer that was 50 miles away. They all said the same thing — that car just isn't available. After hanging up the phone in frustration, I thought, *"OK, Kathy, you can do this the **HARD** way — the way you're going about it now, or you can do this the **EASY** way — allow God to bring it to you. You tried the hard way, now try the easy way."*

I turned around to my computer and typed out:

*"The perfect car is here for me **RIGHT NOW!** God, I thank You for bringing this wonderful car to me. My perfect car is:*

1. A 1992 Bonneville SSEI — it's one year old.
2. The color is white.
3. It has no more than 15,000 miles.
4. I pay no more than $22,000 for it.

THANK YOU, LORD! IT IS DONE!"

I took that piece of paper and taped it to my door, so every day when I came in or left my office I would see it. When I did, I would say, *"Thank You, God, for my new car!"*

A couple of weeks later, late one night, I received a phone call from my friend Chip, who buys and sells nicer cars like Mercedes, Lexus, Jaguar, etc. He was calling me from the auto auction that he attended each week. He said, *"Hey, kiddo, didn't you tell me that you were looking for a 1992 Bonneville SSEI?"*

I got excited! I said, *"Well, yeah. Why do you ask?"*

It Is Done!

He said, *"They're bringing one up on the auction block in a minute. Do you want me to bid on it for you? Let's see, I've got some information on it right here. It's a 1992, has about 15,000 miles on it, and it's white. I can probably get it for about $21,000-$22,000. Should I go for it?"*

> ***1992 BONNEVILLE SSEI***
> *** 15,000 MILES***
> *** WHITE***
> *** $21,000-$22,000***
>
> *** SHOULD HE GO FOR IT? ARE YOU KIDDING?***

And that's how I got the car of my dreams! I drove that car up until 2001 and it was a great car! Believe me, ***NO REQUEST IS TOO SMALL OR TOO LARGE FOR GOD TO HANDLE!*** You can ask for anything! And I mean anything!

THE MIRACLE OF MY *"GETAWAY WEEKEND"*

My school was moving along really well. So well, in fact, that I found myself putting in 60-hour weeks. I was teaching during the week as well as on the weekend, and it was beginning to take a toll on me. I needed a rest!

I decided to take off for the weekend and when I mentioned it to my Dad he gave me a pamphlet that listed all the state-owned parks that included lodging. I perused the pamphlet, picked up the phone, and started calling for a reservation.

There must have been at least 50 parks listed in that pamphlet and I called every single one, only to be told that the lodges were all filled up.

Here I was stressed to the max, which led to my decision to get away. I was getting even more stressed calling all of these lodges and being told *"there was no room in the inn!"*

Finally, after calling the last one listed and being told once again that they were completely booked up, I realized that I had forgotten to ask God to help me. Would I never learn? I laughed and said out loud:

"Lord, You know how badly I need to get away for a weekend. I know one of these lodges has a room available for me and I thank You for bringing it to me RIGHT NOW! ***IT IS DONE!"***

It Is Done!

I took a deep breath, picked up the phone and started at the top of the list. I figured I'd call each lodge and ask if I could be put on a waiting list. The first number I called was for a lodge in Amicalola Falls in Dawsonville, Georgia. I explained that I had called earlier and was informed that they were completely booked for the weekend. Could I put my name on a waiting list in the event someone canceled their reservation?

The woman at the lodge said, *"Well, you picked the right time to call. We just had a cancellation, so a room is available. Shall I sign you up?"*

THANK YOU, LORD!

MIRACLES AT THE AIRPORT

Occasionally I would be asked to do training for an out-of-state lender and on one occasion I traveled to San Antonio, Texas.

When I arrived at the Atlanta airport and checked my luggage at the Delta curbside check-in, I explained to the attendant that I would have to fly into Dallas, Texas and catch a connecting flight to San Antonio. Since the second flight was on a different airline than Delta, would Delta transfer my luggage to the second airline or would I have to go to Baggage Claim in Dallas and pick it up?

I believe this attendant must have been new since he didn't know. He said he'd find out. I don't think he could find anyone to help him so he just came back and told me that my luggage would be transferred.

I was (and still am) in the habit of blessing my luggage and thanking God that it would arrive safely at my destination, so I blessed it and walked to my gate.

The flight to Dallas was delayed and I was getting nervous about making my connecting flight. Would I make it? I said a silent prayer to God, thanking Him for allowing me to make that connecting flight.

Boy did I pray! The delay became greater and greater! When we finally landed at the Dallas airport — *with less than 15 minutes before my connecting flight departed* — I was so thrilled and grateful that the gate for my connecting flight was almost directly across from my arriving

It Is Done!

gate. I took off running and was just barely able to make it onto the flight.

After I got settled on the plane, I began wondering about my luggage. I really didn't see any way that my luggage made the transfer from the Delta flight to the second flight. I figured I'd have to wait at the San Antonio Baggage Claim for the flight arriving right after my flight. Oh well, I knew God was taking care of my luggage so I just released it and relaxed.

Sure enough, my luggage didn't arrive when I did, so I sat down to wait for the next arriving flight from Dallas. A porter came over and asked if I needed help with my luggage and I explained that since my first flight had been delayed, my luggage didn't make the transfer, so I was waiting for the arrival of the next flight.

He questioned me about the airline I had flown in on and I explained I transferred from a Delta flight in Dallas to the commuter flight to San Antonio. He said, *"Delta didn't tell you that you would need to pick up your luggage in Dallas and carry it to the next flight? You know, Delta doesn't transfer luggage if it's not one of their airlines."*

I explained that the attendant at the Delta curbside check-in in Atlanta had assured me that they would. He insisted they wouldn't. He said, *"Ain't no telling where your luggage is now, Miss. I reckon you should go on over to the Delta office and request a tracer, because your luggage ain't comin' in on this next flight!"*

My heart fell. Now what was I going to do? Would the luggage be on the next flight or was it lost somewhere in

Dallas? I took a deep breath and said a silent prayer, *"Lord, I know You're taking care of my luggage and I thank You. I just believe my luggage made it on that next flight and I'm affirming it will be arriving shortly. Thank You, Lord!* ***IT IS DONE!"***

I smiled at the porter and said, *"I guess I'll wait for the next flight and if it's not on there I'll go to the Delta office."*

He kept insisting my luggage was lost somewhere in Dallas and I kept affirming it was on its way! When the luggage began arriving from the next flight I stood up and went over to look for my bag. I watched as most of the luggage made it out of the bin and still didn't see my suitcase. I figured I'd give it just a little longer before I made my way to the Delta office.

All the time I was standing there waiting for my luggage, this porter was telling me, *"Miss, your luggage ain't gonna be on that flight! I'm tellin' you, Delta never transfers luggage to another airline!"*

It was while he was once again telling me that my luggage was still in Dallas that I saw my suitcase come around! I walked over and picked it up, all the time smiling at the porter. I said, *"I guess Delta made an exception this time."*

As I walked away I heard the porter exclaiming to anyone who would listen, *"That's impossible! I ain't never seen Delta transfer luggage to another carrier! I just don't know how that happened!"* **THANK YOU, LORD!**

It Is Done!

Today I travel on a regular basis and I always bless my luggage and thank God for protecting it before I leave on a trip. The only time my luggage has ever been lost is the time I forgot to bless it and thank God for protecting it.

PRAYER – DON'T LEAVE HOME WITHOUT IT!

On another occasion, my flight was scheduled to arrive in Atlanta at about 9 PM but due to weather problems we didn't make it in until after midnight. Unfortunately, I had parked my car close to my home at a hotel that offered a shuttle service to the airport and it stopped running at 11 PM. I'd have to find another way home.

I went to the taxi stand and told the attendant I needed to get to Marietta. Did the taxi drivers take a credit card? Nope — cash only! I looked in my wallet and discovered I only had a $20 bill, which wouldn't be enough to take a taxi home.

I had never been at the airport so late at night and I was uneasy with the interesting characters who were milling around. I heard shouting and turned around to see a man and woman, both obviously drunk, get into a fight — a physical fistfight!

And then a man walked past me with an insolent grin on his face, looking at the diamond ring I was wearing. He said, *"That's a mighty pretty diamond ring you're wearing on your finger (my mother's diamond ring)."* What did that mean? Was this man going to attack me and steal my ring? Where were the police when you needed them?

I said out loud, *"Lord, I do not believe You want me in this place. I know there is a way for me to get home and I thank You NOW for getting me home safely. **IT IS DONE!**"*

At that moment the taxi stand attendant came over to me and said, *"Didn't you say you needed to get to Marietta? Well, this driver has a passenger who is going to Marietta and she's willing to share the fare with you if you're interested. It'll be $15."*

I jumped at the chance! I could pay the driver $15 plus a $5 tip! **THANK YOU, LORD! SAVED AGAIN!**

TRAGEDY STRIKES

I had been living with my Dad for about five years and really enjoying it. My Dad was a very nice man and I had always respected his values and intelligence. He helped me many times over that five-year period when I was sick and in trouble. He was also very open to new spiritual ideas and I loved the time we spent discussing some of the *"alternative"* spiritual philosophies I was learning.

One issue we discussed in great detail was the concept of reincarnation. I had read many books on this topic and asked my Dad to read them and give me his opinion. He told me that the books made a lot of sense and opened up a whole new world for him.

I know he missed my Mother and felt very lonely with her gone. I hoped in some small way that my being there with him kept him from getting depressed. He loved to cook so it was wonderful to come home from a hard day of standing on my feet teaching and sit down to a home-cooked meal. Our deal was that he would cook and I would clean up the kitchen.

I came home from the school one day to find a note from him telling me that he had experienced some bleeding when he urinated so he was driving to the emergency room of our local hospital to have it checked out. The note told me the time he left, which was hours ago, and I began to worry.

I drove over to the emergency room at the hospital to see if I could find him. It took about 30 minutes before I found someone who could help me. He wasn't in the waiting room, but they did have a record that he had been there. It took quite some time to find out what was going on.

It turned out that they diagnosed an enlarged prostate and recommended that he be checked into the hospital for surgery. I tracked him down in his room and spent some time talking to him, trying to find out what was going on.

The prostate surgery was performed within the week. Everyone expected a full recovery. Unfortunately, it didn't turn out that way. He wouldn't stop bleeding and tests revealed that he had a rare blood disease that apparently was untreatable. The only thing they could do was attempt to stop the blood flow and keep him comfortable.

I watched in horror and dismay as this strong, healthy man slowly deteriorated. I visited him every evening after work and on the weekends and did my share of praying, as did my Dad.

One good thing that came out of this tragedy was the reestablishment of my relationship with my older brother, David. David is about two and a half years older than I am and we had lost touch after he left to join the Navy while I was still in high school. His career had taken him to out-of-state locations and he lived in Orlando, Florida at the time. Other than occasional phone calls and an exchange of Christmas or birthday cards, we didn't really speak very often.

When David found out how ill Dad was, he made the long drive several times from Orlando to Atlanta to see him. He stayed at Dad's house with me so it gave us a chance to reestablish our relationship and get to know each other better.

I am so grateful to my brother for all the time and effort he made to be with Dad and me. He was a strong shoulder to cry on while we both watched with sadness as our Dad's health slowly declined.

Dad's illness dragged on for three months with no sign of improvement or hope of recovery. The hospital began discussing placing him in a hospice-type facility.

My brother and I went to look at this facility and were both shocked and dismayed by the dismal environment my Dad would be forced to live in. The walls of the room where he would reside for the rest of his life were painted a nauseating "pea green" and the whole atmosphere was horribly depressing.

I didn't want my Dad living out his final days in a place like that, but allowing him to come home was not an option since he would need constant blood transfusions and other assistance. What to do?

One night while I was mulling over our predicament, I picked up Louise Hay's wonderful book, *"You Can Heal Your Life,"* which I absolutely loved. I flipped to the back of her book to the list of physical problems and the probable emotional cause and looked up *"blood."* This is what her book said:

Blood - *Represents joy in the body, flowing freely.*

Blood Problems - *Lack of joy. Lack of circulation of ideas.*

This was interesting; blood represented joy in the body and blood problems indicated lack of joy. Could this be the issue in my Dad's life? Was there no joy in his life? I suspected that since the death of my Mother in 1987 there had been very little of it.

I spent a sleepless night mulling over what I had read and asking God for guidance as to whether or not I should mention it to my Dad. When I awoke, I had the very distinct feeling that God was giving me the OK to discuss this mind/body connection with him so I decided to take the book with me to the hospital that evening.

I arrived at my Dad's hospital room carrying the book, sat down and told him there was something I wanted to share with him. I showed him the book and explained its contents, pointing to the section in the back that identified physical problems and their probable emotional cause.

I turned to the back of the book and read what it said about blood problems. When I finished reading, I asked my Dad what he thought. He sat there quietly looking at me, then a big tear slid down his cheek. He said, *"It makes sense, doesn't it Kathy? There hasn't been any joy in my life since your Mother died."*

I said, *"You know, Dad, if you want to pass over it's OK."*

He said, *"But I'm worried about you. I need to be here to take care of you, plus, I always thought I'd be here to*

It Is Done!

usher in the new century."

I said, *"You know, Dad, I've been taking care of myself for a long time and, while you've spoiled me while I've been living with you, I'll be OK. I just want you to do what will make you happy. While all of us have been praying for your healing all this time what we should have been praying for is that the outcome is for what is in your highest and best good. To my way of thinking, passing back over to The Other Side isn't a bad thing."*

My Dad said, *"One thing I'm so grateful to you for is asking me to read those books relating to life on The Other Side and reincarnation. They made total sense to me and I have lost all fear of dying. I'm a little scared about the process but I'm not worried at all about what I'll find when I get There. Best of all, I'll be with your Mom again."*

Before I left, my Dad assured me he would think about what we discussed.

When I arrived at his room the next day and sat down to talk to him he reached out and took my hand and said, *"I have something to tell you, I don't know what's going on and I don't want you to tell anyone; they'll think I'm nuts. All day I've been experiencing this strange feeling of floating above the bed. It's almost like I'm floating in the air looking down at myself in the bed. I see myself lying in the bed but I'm seeing only the shell. Maybe I'm hallucinating from the drugs they're giving me; what do you think?"*

I smiled and said, *"Daddy, you're having an out-of-body experience. I've read about it and it seems to happen to lots of people who have been in major accidents or are experiencing a serious illness. What you are doing is 'testing the waters' before you make the decision to pass on or stay.*

"There's nothing to be afraid of and you're definitely not going crazy! Believe it or not, millions of people in America have had out-of-body experiences and they are just now beginning to come forward and share their experiences."

When I left my Dad's hospital room I knew that he was, in fact, testing the waters and trying to decide whether to stay or to go.

I had a pretty good idea that his decision was to pass on, so as soon as I got home I called my brother in Orlando and told him he might want to think about making the trip to Atlanta. I didn't think Daddy would be here much longer. I then called my other brother, Billy, to let him know what was going on.

My Dad passed over within the week. While I missed him terribly, I was so thankful that he was now back on The Other Side with my Mother, where he would experience no more pain and suffering.

I was designated Executor of my Dad's estate and was so fortunate to have two such terrific brothers who were one hundred percent helpful and cooperative in the settling of the estate. Not one harsh word was expressed over the division of any of my Dad's possessions.

It Is Done!

My Dad had purchased a new car less than a year prior to his illness. I knew my younger brother Billy needed a car since his had just broken down and I wondered how my other brother David would feel if Billy got the car. Would he expect some kind of other compensation from the estate if Billy got the car?

While I was mulling over how to approach David about this issue, David called me! He said he knew Billy needed a car; how did I feel about giving him Dad's car?

He made no mention of expecting that he would get something else out of the estate if Billy got the car; he was only thinking about Billy's needs.

Aren't I lucky to have two such great brothers!

THE MIRACLE OF MY NEW HOME

My Dad passed over in September so my brothers and I decided that we would wait until after Thanksgiving and Christmas to put his house up for sale. The holidays were a wonderful time for us, getting reacquainted with each other and our families. I felt so blessed to have such decent and kind brothers and sisters-in-law who were all so helpful in all the many decisions that must be made after a loved one passes.

After the holidays, I put his house on the market, expecting that it would sell quickly since it was in a desirable part of Atlanta. I did an affirmation to God that it would sell quickly, then watched in bewilderment as one month passed, then two, and then a third with no formal offers. I began to wonder what the problem was.

I had done an affirmation and I knew that God always responded very quickly to my request *unless I was doing something to block it.* Was I doing something to block the sale? Did I really want to move?

I hadn't given much thought to what I would do when the house sold but it wasn't something I was terribly worried about; I knew God would provide a place for me to live.

I had a conversation with God, *"Lord, I don't know if it is best for me to stay here or move on, but You do, so I'm asking for Your guidance. If this house doesn't sell by the end of this month I'll consider that confirmation that I should stay here. Thank You, Lord.* ***IT IS DONE!"***

It Is Done!

Within the week, I had a contract on the house! Oh well, I had my answer; it was time for me to move on. The buyers were very accommodating and agreed to allow me two months to find another place and get my loan application processed, so I now set about the task of finding a new place to live.

Once again, I did an affirmation: *"The perfect house is here for me RIGHT NOW, even as I speak! Thank You, Lord, for bringing the perfect house to me. **IT IS DONE!**"*

I selected the area of town that I felt would be a good place for me to live, contacted a Realtor that I knew and instructed her to begin looking for a house. Then I went about my business fully expecting her to find that perfect house for me quickly.

Well, I waited and waited, and my Realtor just couldn't find a house in my price range that I liked. We began our search the first week of March and I really got nervous when I realized that we were already nearing the end of March and I still didn't have one single prospect! I was beginning to panic! I knew it would take about 30 days after I signed my contract to have my loan application processed, and then there would be the scheduling of the loan closing. If I didn't find a house soon I wouldn't be able to meet the deadline for moving out!

Finally, on Wednesday evening, March 30, I sat at my office desk and contemplated the situation. What was going on here? I had affirmed the perfect house and I knew God *ALWAYS* responded immediately — ***unless I was doing something to block it!***

I closed my eyes and asked God for guidance. *"Lord, am I doing something to block my new house? Please give me some guidance."*

I sat quietly with my eyes closed, and the message came: *"Kathy, you are holding on to your Dad's house; you are holding onto the past. It is time to release the past and embrace a new future."*

I had my answer. I recognized that I was holding onto the past and had been unwilling to move forward. I loved my Dad and was having a hard time letting go of a house that he had owned for almost 30 years. That house was the link to my Dad and once that link was severed I guess I feared there was a part of him that I would lose. Just the thought of going through all of his and my Mother's worldly possessions created a knot in my stomach.

I had asked God for advice on whether to keep my Dad's house and live there, or move on. I recognized that God always wanted what was best for me so that meant moving on. I just had to accept it and trust that God was guiding me in the right direction.

I turned around to the computer on my desk and typed:

"I accept that change is good. I release the old and embrace the new! I know the perfect house is here for me RIGHT NOW and I affirm I sign a contract on that perfect house no later than Friday, April 1. Thank You, Lord! ***IT IS DONE!"***

I printed out this affirmation, put my hand on it and repeated the words out loud before I left to go home.

It Is Done!

When I awoke the next morning ***I KNEW EXACTLY WHERE TO LOOK FOR MY PERFECT HOUSE! IT WAS NOWHERE NEAR THE AREA IN WHICH I HAD BEEN LOOKING!***

When I arrived at my office, I immediately called my Realtor. *"Bunny (that was her name), I want you to start looking for a house in the Powers Ferry Road/Terrell Mill Road area."*

Bunny said, *"But that's nowhere near where you told me to look! What made you decide to go to that area?"*

I said, *"I asked God for guidance and when I woke up this morning that was the area in which I was guided to look. I know my house is in that area, Bunny, and I know you're going to find it today! Before we hang up, I want you to repeat after me, 'The perfect house for Kathy is HERE RIGHT NOW and I find it today! Thank You, Lord!* ***IT IS DONE!****'"*

Bunny's response was, *"What?"*

I said, *"I'm serious, Bunny! I want you to repeat those words out loud! This is important! This is my way of affirming that God is finding that perfect house!"*

Bunny mumbled, *"Well, I'll do the best I can."*

I said, *"No, no, no! You must repeat these words, 'The perfect house for Kathy is HERE RIGHT NOW and I find it today! Thank You, Lord!* ***IT IS DONE!****'"*

Bunny responded, *"This is really weird, Kathy. I don't*

feel comfortable saying that."

I said, *"Bunny, trust me! The quicker you repeat these words, the quicker you will find my house! Humor me! Please repeat these words!"*

I finally convinced Bunny to repeat the words, which she mumbled, before she hung up the phone.

Less than an hour after I talked to her, Bunny was back on the phone to me. She sounded very strange, as if she was in shock, and she stumbled over her words: *"Kathy, uh, this is Bunny. Well, I, uh, looked up some houses in the Multiple Listing Service (MLS) in the area you told me to look, and uh, well, I, uh, got in my car and drove over to look at one, and, uh, well, I think I found your house."*

I was so excited! *"Really! Where is it?"*

Bunny gave me the address and directions to the house and I got in my car and took off! This was great; the house was ten minutes from my office! I never dreamed that I would find a house so close to my office!

As I followed Bunny's directions and turned onto the street she had indicated, I saw her standing by her car in front of — Oh, my gosh! ***SHE WAS STANDING IN FRONT OF MY HOUSE! I JUST KNEW IT WAS MY HOUSE!***

I pulled up behind her car, got out and began walking toward her. Bunny had a very strange look on her face — the look was fear! I think Bunny thought I was a witch or something! When I walked up to her she kept looking from

It Is Done!

me to the house and back to me, looking for a sign she had *"done good."*

She said, *"This house was just listed this week. When I saw the listing in the MLS, I just had a feeling I should take a look at it. The minute I pulled up in front I just had this feeling it was your house. When I went in and looked at it, I just had a feeling it was your house...I'm babbling I know. It's just that I feel funny...does what I'm saying make any sense to you?"*

I was hardly paying attention to what Bunny was saying; I was gazing in awe at this wonderful house that I knew was my house! It sat on a 3/4 acre shaded corner lot and it was obvious that the owners took a great deal of pride in maintaining the beautifully landscaped yard. Azalea bushes were blooming in abundance in the front and back yard, and there was a beautiful magnolia tree in the front yard in full bloom.

The house was brick on all four sides. It had a living room, formal dining room, small eat-in kitchen, small den with a fireplace, and three bedrooms and two baths on the main level. The master bedroom was huge; it looked like the owners had removed the wall between two bedrooms to make one large master bedroom.

Downstairs there was a huge family room with a wet bar and fireplace, plus two more bedrooms, a full bath, laundry room, and a two-car drive-under garage. It was perfect! The asking price was $143,600 — well below my targeted price of no more than $150,000!

After slowly touring the house with Bunny, I looked at her, smiled, and said, *"Bunny, you done good!"* I wrote a contract on it that very day and it was signed by the sellers the next day! I had, indeed, found the perfect house and signed a contract no later than April 1, just as I had affirmed!

My next door neighbor, Minnie, later told me that when she saw the "For Sale" sign go up she immediately called her sister, who was looking for a house in that neighborhood. Both she and her sister made several unsuccessful attempts to contact the homeowners. By the time she reached them, they had already signed a contract with me!

I was sorry that Minnie's sister missed the opportunity to buy the house but as I told her, *"Minnie, the reason you couldn't reach the owners is because God saved this house for ME!"*

Over the years both Minnie and her husband, Bob, have turned out to be wonderful neighbors and I'm very blessed to have them living next door. They are both kindhearted, hard working, honest people who go out of their way to help me in any way they can.

Eight years later I still live in that house! I added a wood deck along the entire back of the house and installed French doors in the kitchen, middle bedroom (which is my home office) and the master bedroom. The pleasure I take in sitting out there and viewing my magnificent wooded back yard is beyond words.

THANK YOU, LORD!

THE MIRACLE OF MY NEW OFFICE

During the time I was looking for a new house I was also looking for new office space. I had been in my current office space for five years and my lease was up.

My mortgage-training institute had been doing very well and I needed to expand my office space from about 2,000 to about 3,000 square feet. Unfortunately my landlord couldn't accommodate me in my current building, so I had a Tenant Rep out looking for new space.

Of course, I did my affirmation for the perfect office space and it wasn't long before my Tenant Rep found a space that met all of my requirements. We began the negotiations, agreed on everything, and submitted the lease agreement to the landlord for approval and signatures.

Typically a lease agreement is signed by the landlord and returned to the prospective tenant for signature within days of all parties agreeing to the terms of the lease, but this time the landlord was dragging his feet signing the lease.

It was so unusual for this to happen and my Tenant Rep continually called me to express his bewilderment over this occurrence.

In my experience with positive affirmations, I went on the premise that God *ALWAYS* responded immediately — unless I was doing something to block it *OR THERE WAS SOMETHING BETTER OUT THERE.*

In this instance I didn't feel I was doing anything to block moving to a new space so I believed that there was something better available. I told my Tenant Rep, *"Craig, don't worry about it. It's just possible that God has a better space available for us. Let's just see what happens."*

Finally I received a call from my Tenant Rep informing me that the landlord had signed the lease — he would come over to my office that afternoon to get my signature. I had no sooner hung up the phone than my Receptionist called to tell me my current landlord's leasing agent, Joe, was in the lobby wanting to see me — ***IMMEDIATELY!*** What was this all about?

I walked into the lobby and asked Joe what I could do for him. Joe blurted out, *"Have you signed your lease for the new space yet?"*

I told him my Tenant Rep was coming over that afternoon to get my signature.

Joe pleaded, *"Please don't sign that lease until you talk to Mr. Cho (my landlord). He has a space he wants to show you in his other building. Please, Kathy, won't you at least take a look at it?"*

Knowing how delays in getting my affirmations answered usually led to something better, I agreed to hold off signing the lease until I looked at the space. I called my Tenant Rep and laughingly told him what happened and he responded, *"Boy, this is really cutting it close! Did Mr. Cho know you were signing the lease today? I mean, it's so strange that he had to see you the very day we got the signed lease back, isn't it?"*

It Is Done!

I assured him I'd be in touch after looking at the office space, and drove over to Mr. Cho's other office building right around the corner. The space Mr. Cho showed me was wonderful and even included my own private balcony! It had a breathtaking view of the Atlanta skyline, plus the building was in an even better location than the space I was negotiating.

There was just one problem. The space Mr. Cho showed me was over 5,000 square feet and I was planning on leasing only 3,000 square feet; there was no way I could afford that much office space!

I broke out in a cold sweat just thinking about the prospect of tripling my monthly expenditure!

I guess it pays to be a good tenant who always pays one's rent on time because Mr. Cho offered me a terrific deal on the space. I told Mr. Cho I wanted 24 hours to think about it, and believe me I spent a sleepless night wondering what I was getting myself into!

The issue that kept running through my mind was the delay in getting the lease on the other space signed only to have Mr. Cho offer me this space right before I signed my new lease; it appeared that this new space was a blessing from God. That's what really helped me make my decision. I would go for the new space trusting that God would take care of me and make sure the money was available to pay the rent.

As a matter of fact, the building that contained the office space I was negotiating on ended up being torn down and replaced by a car dealership! I never would have made it through my five-year lease!

I took a big leap in faith and signed a five-year lease for this huge office space. After all, my business was really doing well, wasn't it? And anything I wanted I only had to affirm it and I got it. I'd just affirm more business to pay for the larger office space.

No problem!

Boy was I in for a big surprise! What's the old saying, *"Pride cometh before a fall."* And was I ever in for a big fall!

MY WORLD FALLS APART

In my spiritual quest I had read many books on prosperity which explained that I should *"Claim my good. Imagine my good. Speak the word for my good. **Then care not if my good ever comes to pass."***

This is basically saying that I am to have an attitude of non-resistance or *"Let go and let God."* Of course, letting God do anything in my life is also understanding that God can only work ***through me to the extent I ALLOW*** — this is known as Free Will.

Many years after the horrible experiences happened to me that I'll share with you, I have learned that it is possible for anyone to make positive affirmations and receive whatever one affirms.

Unfortunately, if we don't first establish a true consciousness of *"non-resistance,"* we basically short-circuit the system and it backfires. Especially if our subconscious mind is full of lack and limitation!

I was raised by parents who were truly wonderful but we never had much money. My formative years were spent scrimping and saving for everything; it was a poverty mentality that I must have brought forward to my adult life.

I felt guilty making a lot of money. It's that simple. Despite my arrogant assertion that *"I could have the desires of my heart,"* deep down the fear was gnawing at me that it wouldn't last, I didn't deserve it, I wasn't good enough...we've all had these thoughts.

And since ***"Thoughts are Things,"*** despite all my hard-earned success I ended up where I truly believed I belonged — ***WITH NOTHING!***

Although I believed at that time that I had a *"Prosperity Consciousness,"* in reality my true consciousness was one of fear, lack, and limitation. I was relying on the mental work of spouting positive affirmations, rather than building on a true spiritual consciousness and connection to the Higher Power. I fell flat on my face.

I moved into my new office space in May of 1994 at a time when interest rates had dropped dramatically. Homeowners were clamoring to refinance their mortgage to a lower rate, so everyone was trying to get into the mortgage business to cash in on the refinance boom. My classes were packed.

Then interest rates leveled out and began to rise. The increase in interest rates was a very small one but it was enough to bring the mortgage industry to a screeching halt. About one-third of the mortgage companies in Atlanta shut their doors while others were scrambling to merge with each other to stay afloat. My business stopped dead.

I didn't have enough students to even pay the rent, let alone pay my employees and all other expenses. I was forced to lay off all of my employees except one. I had to contact all of my creditors and alert them to the situation, asking them to work with me. It was humiliating, to say the least. My pride was sorely bruised since I had always maintained an impeccable credit rating, but I was relieved to find that all of my creditors were willing to give me an opportunity to work things out.

It Is Done!

My landlord, Mr. Cho, was the last one I contacted. It was the hardest thing I've ever done in my life to explain to him that I would be unable to pay the monthly rent; would he be willing to work with me until I got back on my feet? Although he was very angry that I had apparently bitten off more than I could chew, he grudgingly agreed to reduce my monthly rent.

I had a little bit of money left to me from my Dad's estate, which is what I lived off of until I could get things back on track. It was the loneliest time of my life.

I was ashamed to tell anyone what had happened since I was the one running around spouting positive affirmations; I felt sure they would love to see me fall flat on my face. I didn't have a boyfriend at that time, I had no parents I could talk to, and I hid the truth from my friends.

I was right back where I started way back in 1986 when I first established my school. All of those years of hard work and I had come full circle — right back to the lack and limitation I felt I deserved.

I was exhausted from running around trying to appease my creditors, trying to reason with my landlord, trying to figure out ways to generate some business, and trying to find jobs for the employees I had to lay off. It took about 90 days for everything to settle down and allow for a small breather.

No sooner had I resolved all of these issues when I received a certified letter from the IRS — ***THIS WAS NOT GOOD!*** Apparently my bookkeeper had failed to pay my last quarterly payroll taxes.

When I discussed it with her she simply stated, *"Well, I knew you were going through a really hard time and I didn't want to burden you with another problem."*

If she had come to me and asked me how we were going to pay the payroll taxes, I could have taken the money out of the private funds my Dad had left me; it was only about $15,000. Unfortunately, delinquent payroll tax penalties are outrageous and by the time I got the certified letter I didn't owe $15,000 — I owed over $45,000! There was no way I could come up with that kind of money! Only the government is permitted to charge a late penalty which is triple the amount you originally owed!

The IRS slapped a tax lien on me (there went my impeccable credit rating) and used their Gestapo threats of shutting me down and throwing me in jail. I had to hire an attorney to negotiate a payment plan.

After two very long months of negotiations, the IRS finally agreed to a payment plan that didn't bankrupt me every month and I breathed a sigh of relief. However, my relief was short-lived.

No sooner had I settled with the IRS than I received a certified letter (I hate certified letters!) from the attorney representing the lumber company demanding payment of the $50,000 debt on which my ex-husband had defaulted.

I couldn't believe it! It had been over four years since the original notice and I thought we had resolved the issue.

Apparently the attorneys representing the lumber company convinced them to pursue collection through me,

It Is Done!

since the "ex" was no longer in the state and their attempts to reach him had failed. I was right back where I started with them! I had to hire another attorney to represent me in this suit, which depleted my meager savings even more!

Could things get any worse? I dreaded getting out of bed every morning. I dreaded going to work for fear that I'd be hit with another major crisis. I dreaded going home at night, being alone and just thinking about all the problems I was facing.

I kept asking myself what went wrong. I had done all of the positive affirmations and they really worked. Why weren't they working now? At that time I had no true understanding of the spiritual concepts I would learn later and I was in no mood to pursue them. I was much too busy wallowing in self-pity to attempt to seek out the answers.

I struggled for over a year trying to get back on track and the final blow came when my landlord's leasing agent came into my office one day and said, *"Kathy, Mr. Cho would like you to start paying the full amount of your monthly rent now; it's been a year and he feels it's time to get back on track. We also need to talk about how you intend to pay back the monthly rental you've been deferring."*

What else could go wrong, I thought. Then all of a sudden, I felt a sense of peace I had not felt before. From somewhere inside of me I heard, *"Kathy, just let it go."* And I did. I said, *"You know, Joe, you're absolutely right. Mr. Cho has been wonderful this past year and it's time to start paying the full rent. As for the amount I've deferred,* *would it be OK if I pay an additional $1,000 per month until we're caught up?"*

Joe smiled and said, *"I'm sure that will be OK with Mr. Cho. You've really worked hard to keep your business going and I'm sure you'll be just fine."*

I had no idea where the money was coming from but I realized that, despite everything that had happened to me over the past year or so, things had worked out OK. I silently said to God, *"You know, Lord, everything has worked out so far; I still have a nice house to live in, a nice car to drive, and an office to come to every day. When I run around trying to fix things on my own, that's when I get sideswiped. When I relax and turn the details over to you, everything works out as it should."*

This was a major insight for me. God was waiting for me to acknowledge that all would be well, instead of dwelling on what all could go wrong. It's the old **"THOUGHTS ARE THINGS"** issue and dwelling on negative things attracted negative back.

When I acknowledged that everything would work out, I was thanking God in advance, trusting that all would be well. And so it was. It's just a shame that it took me over a year to realize it! I could have saved myself a lot of heartache!

It Is Done!

GOD GIVES ME A SIGN THAT THINGS WILL GET BETTER

It had been over a year since my world fell apart and still I didn't see any light at the end of the tunnel. On top of everything else, I got pneumonia again but still had to drag myself out of bed and drive seven hours to Tampa, Florida to teach a class. There was no way I could cancel the class — I was lucky that a bank had called and asked me to teach a class for them and I needed the money!

I pulled out Louise Hay's book, *"You Can Heal Your Life,"* and went to her list of physical ailments in the back to see what the emotional cause of pneumonia was. It said, *"Desperate. Tired of life. Emotional wounds that are not allowed to heal."*

Yup; that pretty much summed up my life at that time! I told God, *"You know, Lord, I would never commit suicide since I know there are lessons I need to learn, but I must tell You, I can understand why people choose that way out."*

A friend of mine who lived in a small town in Texas coaxed me into flying out to spend a few days with her and her family. Despite my protestations that I couldn't afford it and couldn't take off the time, she convinced me that I needed to take a little breather and recuperate from the pneumonia. Also, it wouldn't hurt to distance myself from everything that was going on.

I spent a relaxing long weekend with my friend and her family and it was with much regret that I gathered my things together to make the flight home. I had to fly on a small ten-seater commuter plane that would take me to the Dallas airport for my connecting flight to Atlanta, and my friend and her husband joked about the "puddle jumper" I was flying on. I boarded the plane and settled in my seat with the other seven or eight people on the flight.

After we were airborne I pulled out my book and began reading. Shortly after our takeoff we ran into a bad thunderstorm and the plane began swaying and diving dramatically. Several times my stomach ended up in my throat when it seemed that the plane was going to fall out of the sky!

I glanced around at the other people on the flight and saw all of them clinging to their seats, white knuckles very much in evidence. Was I scared? Probably a little, but the thought of crashing really didn't frighten me. I told God, *"You know, Lord, the worst thing that can happen is that we crash and I die. What's so bad about passing back over to The Other Side? At this point in my life it would be a relief!"*

I calmed my fear and went back to reading my book, and eventually the storm abated and the plane settled down. I continued reading my book but felt a strange prickling sensation on the back of my neck. I looked up to see if anything was going on; all of the passengers seemed to be dozing or reading. What was going on here? I went back to reading my book.

Once again, I felt a strange prickling on the back of my neck and looked up again. Still nothing seemed to be out of the ordinary. Was I missing something? I lowered my head to continue reading my book when I felt a strange compunction, almost a command, to look out the window.

I glanced out the window at the dark thunderclouds that surrounded the plane, wondering where this feeling was coming from. Suddenly the clouds parted — and I gazed in awe ***AT THE MOST MAGNIFICENT RAINBOW I HAD EVER SEEN!***

I was overwhelmed! I had never seen a rainbow so close, nor had I ever realized how totally alive its colors were! I quickly glanced around at the other passengers on the plane to get their reaction. Apparently nobody else saw it!

I leaned forward and started to tell one of the other passengers to look out the window at the magnificent rainbow when I stopped. I heard a voice very gently speak to me, *"No, Kathy, this is not for them. This is for you. All will be well."*

I was overwhelmed with emotion. God was very much aware of the trials and tribulations I had been going through and He was letting me know that everything was going to be OK. I stared at that rainbow until it disappeared from sight.

THANK YOU, LORD!

THE MIRACLE OF MY SCHOOL'S NEW DIRECTION

I arrived back in Atlanta with a renewed sense of well being. I knew that everything was going to be OK and went back to work with a feeling of anticipation. It didn't take long!

Two days after I returned to my office in Atlanta I received a phone call from a former student who lived in New York. This gentleman had taken my course in Atlanta many years previously before moving back to New York. He called me quite often with questions regarding FHA loans.

On several occasions he put me on the speakerphone to argue with his underwriter about an FHA issue that the two were disputing.

It was obvious to me every time I talked to someone in New York regarding an FHA issue that New Yorkers were not very knowledgeable on this type of financing, so I was delighted when this gentleman called me after once again arguing with his FHA underwriter and suggested that I consider teaching a class on FHA financing procedures in New York.

Teach a class in New York on FHA financing procedures — now why didn't I think of that? I had been living in a fog, trying to keep my head above water for about a year and a half without giving much thought to how I could increase business. Once again, God stepped in and helped me out!

It Is Done!

This gentleman wanted to make sure I taught that class in New York so he contacted everyone he knew and made a concerted effort to market the class. I ended up with over 50 students in my first class!

The response was so overwhelmingly positive that I began receiving calls from mortgage companies in New York asking when I would be doing another class. That was the start of an entirely new market for me and I began scheduling classes on a regular basis.

Phone calls started coming in from mortgage companies in New Jersey asking for FHA training, so I began scheduling classes in New Jersey. Then I received a call from a mortgage company in Baltimore, Maryland asking if I would offer the class in Baltimore, so I began offering the class there as well.

Within six months my out-of-state classes were generating enough money to pay for my overhead and I was able to hire an individual to market to these out-of-state locations.

On one occasion she asked me to take a phone call from a man in New York who was being quite rude to her. That was puzzling; why was he being so rude?

When I took the call and asked how I could help, the gentleman said that he was calling to sign up for the FHA class we were offering that month in New York. He said, *"I just want you to know that I don't appreciate being forced to take this class."*

I was bewildered. *"I'm sorry, I don't understand what you mean. Who is making you take this class?"*

He snarled, *"I tried to sign up with the New York FHA office to take the test to become an FHA Direct Endorsement Underwriter and they told me I couldn't sign up to take the test unless I showed proof that I had been through your class. What kind of deal do you have with them anyway?"*

I was still puzzled. *"I'm afraid I don't know what you're talking about. Who at FHA told you that you had to take my class and how did anyone at FHA even know about the class I teach up there?"*

He said, *"I don't know how they know about your class but that's what they're telling everyone. I talked to a guy named ―――."*

I explained that I knew nothing about this requirement from the New York FHA office but I assured him that the class would be very valuable if he wanted to become an FHA underwriter.

When I hung up the phone I sat there wondering about what he had told me. I still didn't understand how anyone at FHA even knew about the class I was teaching in New York and I certainly didn't understand how they were requiring everyone to take my class when I had never even discussed my class with anyone at FHA.

FHA is a government agency; what were my chances of getting through to the man whose name I had written down? Oh well, I might as well start trying to locate him. It took about an hour to finally get through.

I introduced myself and explained that I was very grateful that they were referring people to my class. Then I asked him how he had heard about the class.

He responded, *"Well, we began to notice that there were a number of people taking our examination to become an FHA underwriter who were receiving much higher scores than we've ever seen before and we started wondering how they were able to do so well.*

"When we called these people back and questioned them about how they were able to score so highly, it appeared that they had all been through your training. It just made sense to us that if we wanted qualified FHA underwriters, then they needed to attend your class, so we decided to make attendance mandatory."

Wow! That was quite a compliment coming from a government agency! I thanked him for his support and offered the class to anyone at FHA who would be interested in attending. From that point forward I always had many FHA employees in the class, which added credibility.

When I look back on the horrible experience I went through, I realize now that it could be considered **"The Worst of Times AND The Best of Times."** If my business had continued doing well in Atlanta, I never would have considered traveling out-of-state to conduct classes.

Because the business got so bad in Atlanta I was forced to expand my training to other locations, which gained a national recognition for my school that I never would have achieved otherwise as well as increasing my income far and above anything I could have generated if I had limited myself to training only in Atlanta. I am constantly reminded that ***"All things work for good to those who trust in God."***

I MEET THE MAN OF MY DREAMS

It had been almost two years since the collapse of my business and I had worked long, hard hours trying to build it back up. As a matter of fact, work was all I was doing! I had one Receptionist and one person who marketed classes for me — that was it! I was having to write all of the course manuals, design the courses, teach all the classes, handle all the business...in other words, I was working about 12 hours a day 7 days a week!

One Saturday I taught a class all day, then went home and collapsed. At about 7 PM I received a phone call from a friend of mine that I had known since high school. She and several of her friends were going out dancing and she called to see if I would like to join them.

I informed her that I was exhausted from teaching all day and really didn't feel like going out; I'd take a rain check. Despite her efforts to convince me to go, I just didn't feel up to it.

About an hour after I spoke to her, she called me back. She said, *"I've been thinking about you and I think you've been working way too hard, Kathy. You need a little fun in your life. So here's the deal — if you won't drive to the nightclub to meet us, I'm driving to your house to get you. So what's it gonna be? Will you meet us later or will I have to come get you?"*

I laughed and said, *"OK, OK, Barbara. You're right, I do need a break. Tell you what, let me take a little nap and I'll meet you there about 10 PM. Is that OK?"*

We agreed that I would meet her there and I decided to rest awhile first. When I awoke at about 9 PM, I still felt groggy so I took a nice relaxing shower, got dressed and drove to the nightclub to meet her and her friends.

When I arrived, it took a few minutes to locate the group, but I quickly settled in and started to relax. Several people asked me to dance and I was really enjoying myself. One man in particular asked me to dance a couple of times and we spent a little time trying to talk to each other over the loud music. He complained that the music was a little distracting and suggested that we drive to another local nightclub that was a little quieter.

I really didn't feel comfortable leaving with someone I didn't know, so I gave him my business card and casually suggested he call me sometime.

He left and I didn't give it much thought. I figured I'd never see him again. I met another nice man and spent the rest of the evening dancing and talking to him. We left the nightclub and walked across the street to a diner for breakfast. I didn't get home until about 4 AM! I couldn't believe I stayed out that late and decided I'd sleep that whole Sunday.

About 10 AM my phone rang — it was the man I met earlier the previous night, calling to invite me to brunch! How did he get my home phone number? It turned out that he looked up my name in the phone book and kept calling everyone named Kathy Lewis until he got the right one.

I was still groggy from staying out so late and I suggested that we have dinner rather than brunch, so we made arrangements to meet that evening at a local restaurant. I had a surprisingly pleasant evening with this man and found that I was very comfortable around him.

He called me the next day and offered to cook dinner at my house. I was sold — any man who would cook for me (since I didn't cook) had a clear path to my heart!

From that point forward we seemed to spend almost every day together and the relationship was one of the most comfortable ones I had ever experienced.

Perhaps we didn't have the mad, passionate feelings that some people seek but by the time I reached my mid-40s, I had been through my share of passion and pathos; I'd take a comfortable, satisfying relationship with a wonderful man any day over the passion.

My high school girlfriend who talked me into meeting her that night told me later that she didn't know why she felt compelled to force me to go unless God was using her as my guardian angel to guide me to Garry. To this day she tells everyone that it was because of her that I met him and I'm more than happy to give her the credit!

Garry's background was sales and he saw a real opportunity in the mortgage business, so he decided to attend my school. While he was attending, he began making suggestions for ways to increase my business and eventually suggested that he come to work with me.

I flew into a panic! I'd been through one business/marriage relationship that was a total disaster! Was I prepared to risk that again?

What happened if he did a terrible job? How would it affect our personal relationship? What if our personal relationship didn't work out? How would it affect our business relationship?

One night I was unable to sleep worrying about this issue, so I got up and went into my darkened den, sat down and asked God for guidance. *"What should I do, Lord? Should I allow him to come into my business? Should I keep our business and personal relationship separate? Please give me an answer."*

As I sat there in the darkness, a thought popped into my head: *"I will give you the desires of your heart."*

Yes, Lord, you have given me the desires of my heart many, many times. What is my heart's desire? As I thought about it, I realized that all my adult life I recognized that I was born to be a businesswoman and always had a desire for a man in my life who could share my business as well as my personal life.

That was my true heart's desire. God was telling me He would give me the desires of my heart. I made the decision that life was too short to live in fear. I'd go for it.

I told Garry the next day that I had made the decision to allow him to work in my business with me and it turned out to be a very good decision.

Garry and I have been together over six years and spend 24 hours a day, 7 days a week together. To date we have had no major arguments and have hardly ever spoken harsh words to each other. It's turned out to be a wonderful relationship.

I spent years and years in relationships with men who constantly put me down, berated me, and told me what a "nothing" I was. As I grew spiritually I recognized that these men were only repeating out loud what I felt about myself. Since ***"Thoughts are Things,"*** I was attracting through my thoughts the very men who would reinforce the way I felt about myself.

When I recognized that I didn't want that kind of relationship with a man, I realized that it was best to forego dating men until I did a little more growing spiritually. I wanted to get to the point in my life where I saw myself as God saw me.

When I truly liked, no, when I truly *loved* myself and saw value in me as an individual soul I would then attract a man in my life who also loved me and saw value in me.

Garry shows me every day how much he loves and cherishes me. All of my friends and employees marvel at how well he takes care of me and caters to my every wish. He's constantly cooking things I will enjoy or planning trips that we can share together and I'm truly blessed with this wonderful man.

MY SCHOOL EXPANDS IN YET ANOTHER DIRECTION

With Garry's help, my school continued to grow and expand. The downside of this tremendous growth was that I was traveling on the road constantly. Just about every single month I traveled to one city or another and it was really starting to wear me down. On one particular occasion I taught a class in Dallas, Texas and would leave Dallas and fly to New Jersey to teach a class.

Thank Heaven, Garry was with me. On that particular occasion we arrived at the Dallas airport at 8 AM for a flight to New Jersey. We finally arrived in our hotel room in New Jersey at 8 PM that night! We were at the airport all day long due to delays and it was an incredibly stressful and exhausting day!

That night I told God, *"Lord, I'm so tired of traveling! I know it seems like I'm never happy despite all the wonderful blessings You shower on me! I should be grateful for all the business You send my way, and instead I'm complaining.*

"Nevertheless, there must be another direction I can take that will get me off the road! I know there is a way to do it, Lord, and I thank You for leading me in that direction. Thank You, Lord! ***IT IS DONE!"***

As soon as I say the words ***"IT IS DONE!"*** Spirit immediately responds! On the plane back to Atlanta, an idea popped into my head: *"Why not produce videos and sell video training? That would keep me off the road but*

It Is Done!

still generate the income I would lose if I stopped traveling! What a great idea! Thank You, Lord!"

I shared my idea with Garry and he set about the task of finding out everything he could about setting up our own video recording studio. I knew the only way I could generate videos would be to produce them in our own studio, since mortgage industry guidelines are constantly changing.

I could just see myself spending $50,000 to produce a training video only to have the mortgage lending guidelines change even before the video was edited! If we had our own studio we could make the necessary changes right there.

In researching what it would take to set up our own studio we received quotes ranging everywhere from $150,000 to $500,000 and even higher! I thought that was nuts and honestly believed that we would be able to set up our own video recording studio for substantially less than that.

I realized that I had gone into this search without doing my usual ***positive affirmation***, so after spending several unsuccessful months searching for the right person to help us set up a studio I sat down and did my affirmation: *"Lord, I know there is a way to set up this video recording studio with quality equipment at a fair and reasonable price and I thank You for bringing to me the person who can do it for us. Thank You, Lord!* ***IT IS DONE!"***

Sure enough, it wasn't two days later that one of my employees came to me with the name of a company she had gotten off the internet that could put together our entire recording studio. The owner of this company was absolutely wonderful and offered us a terrific deal on all of the equipment we would need to get up and running.

I knew that it would be tough to give up the revenue I was making from my out-of-state classes but I also knew that the income would eventually be replaced by the sales of my videos.

The money paid out for the video recording studio, coupled with the reduction in revenue from not doing out-of-state classes eventually put us in a financial bind. I knew I was in trouble when I had to withdraw money from a line of credit to make payroll!

I had always run my business without borrowing money and now I found myself having to draw from that line of credit on more than one occasion just to meet our monthly bills and it would be several months before the videos were ready for sale! We were in trouble!

THE MIRACLE OF THE PRAYER OF GRATITUDE — GETTING MY EMPLOYEES INVOLVED

For the third month in a row I was forced to transfer funds from a line of credit to meet our monthly expenses and I knew something had to be done. Garry and I discussed it and he felt the only way out was to lay off two or three employees. I had a wonderful staff that had taken me years to assemble and that was not the route I wanted to take.

I went into meditation to think about my options:

- I could lay off some employees to reduce my monthly overhead, or

- I could schedule an out-of-state class and go back on the road.

Neither one of these options appealed to me and I found myself in a real dilemma. Being a martyr and victim by nature I decided the only route to take was to go back on the road and suffer through the trials and tribulations of travel.

I really didn't feel I had any other choice since I had allowed **FEAR** to cloud my spiritual judgment. I started remembering those horrible two years when my business struggled to keep afloat and all I could see was the same thing happening all over again! The panic and fear continued to build day after day until I finally came into my office, closed the door, and had a conversation with God:

*"Lord, I refuse to fall back into that fear and panic I experienced before! **THIS SITUATION IS TOTALLY UNACCEPTABLE!** There comes a point in my life where **I EITHER BELIEVE OR I DON'T! IT'S THAT SIMPLE!***

*"I know doing the videos is the right thing and I know the income from videos will eventually surpass what I made in out-of-state classes. I also recognize that I have wonderful employees and absolutely don't want to let any of them go! So I'm trusting that You will provide the income needed to keep this company going **WITHOUT MY HAVING TO GO BACK ON THE ROAD!** Thank You, Lord! **IT IS DONE!**"*

I then called all of my employees together for a meeting. I could tell from the looks on their faces that they anticipated some of them would be laid off; they knew we were hurting financially. I opened the meeting by saying:

"You know, guys, we've been experiencing some financial problems and I've been so wrapped up in these problems that I forgot to give thanks to God for what we do have! Every phone call that comes into this school is a Gift from God. Do you agree?

*"I believe that we have been negligent in thanking God for the many, many blessings He's directed to this school, so here's what we are going to do. Every single time that phone rings I want each and every one of you to say **OUT LOUD, 'Thank You, Lord'!**"*

It Is Done!

All of my employees looked at each other and then looked at me as if to say I had lost my mind. They weren't understanding what I was saying.

I repeated, *"Every time that phone rings I want each and every one of you to say **OUT LOUD**, 'Thank You, Lord'. We have one of two choices here: I can lay off some of you or we can accept that God is providing all of the business we can handle. What's it gonna be? It's your choice!"*

One of my employees said, *"You want us to say this **OUT LOUD**?"*

I said, *"Yup! **OUT LOUD**! And I want to hear EACH AND EVERY ONE OF YOU SAYING IT TOGETHER! Are you all clear on this? You know that God ALWAYS provides, therefore we will thank Him for every phone call that comes in here! Let's get to work!"*

All of my employees knew that I embraced spiritual principles but I believe they thought I was taking it to the extreme this time. Fortunately, they valued their jobs enough to give it a try, so when the phone rang the next time I started running up and down the hall yelling, **"THANK YOU, LORD!** *Let's hear it, guys!* **THANK YOU, LORD!"**

I heard them mumble a half-hearted *"Thank You, Lord"* and I jokingly yelled out, **"I CAN'T HEAR YOU! LOUDER!"**

They started laughing and yelled out, **"THANK YOU, LORD!"**

From that day forward, every time the phone rang my entire staff yelled out in unison, *"THANK YOU, LORD!"* And a wonderful thing happened — *OUR PHONES BEGAN TO RING OFF THE HOOK!...AND THEY KEPT RINGING!*

All of our classes were completely filled up that month and have continued to fill up every month!

It Is Done!

THE MIRACLE OF GETTING COLLEGE ACCREDITATION

One day we received an out-of-state phone call from a gentleman who was a recently retired College Dean. Some friends of his who owned a mortgage company discussed having him come to work with them and suggested that he attend our school to learn the mortgage business.

He requested one of our catalogues and after reviewing the information it hit him that our courses would in all likelihood qualify for college accreditation. He called to see if we would be interested in pursuing the accreditation and offered his expertise to put together the application.

With his help, we were able to receive college accreditation for our courses and the first university has begun offering a two-year Associate of Business and Science Degree in Mortgage Finance!

College accreditation opens up a whole new world for the school and we hope to work with many other colleges to offer our courses for a degree!

The gentleman who helped us receive our accreditation is also a minister whom I believe was led by God to help us in this endeavor. ***Thank You, Lord!***

Isn't it amazing how these *"coincidences"* keep happening?

AFFIRMING A *"COMPUTER GEEK"* TO HELP WITH A TECHNICAL ISSUE

Part of the service my school provides to students and mortgage professionals is the opportunity to call us at any time to have their technical questions answered, most of which relate to FHA loans.

FHA lender guidelines can be very confusing and trying to get answers to your questions can be frustrating and time-consuming since most of FHA's guideline changes are issued in the form of memos rather than handbook updates.

I got the idea of creating a database of these FHA memos and handbooks tied to a search engine that would allow an individual to simply type in a word and be taken directly to the specific memo or handbook that explained it.

One of my staff members had a Masters Degree in Computer Science, so I gave him the task of setting up the database and sat back and waited...and waited...and waited.

Every time I asked him how he was progressing, his response was, *"I'm gettin' there!"*

His *"gettin' there"* dragged on for almost a year and I still didn't see any completion in sight. I decided it was time to take action.

It Is Done!

I had begun attending a weekly Prayer Circle offered at a local metaphysical bookstore and in one particular meeting we decided to write down something we wanted and have the group *"affirm"* it. Since I am a strong believer in the power of positive affirmations, I eagerly wrote down my desire: *"I affirm the perfect 'computer geek' is here to get my FHA database up and running quickly."*

I read my affirmation to the group and they all affirmed it. That was on a Wednesday night.

The following Monday morning my receptionist informed me that she had a caller on the line who was inquiring about the computer programmer position we were advertising. I said, *"What computer position? We're not running an ad. He probably has the wrong number...wait a minute! Did you say he was a computer professional? I'll take that call!"*

I answered the call and questioned the man. He said he was responding to our ad in the local newspaper for a computer programmer and I explained that we had no such ad running. I asked him what telephone number he was calling and he had, in fact, dialed the wrong number.

I said, *"Well, you did dial the wrong number but while I have you on the phone let me explain to you what I'm looking for."* I then told him what we were trying to accomplish and asked if he knew of anyone who could handle it for us. Sure enough, he knew of a company that could perform the function we needed!

He was kind enough to call me back with the company name and telephone number and I immediately dialed the number when I hung up. I spoke with the owner and explained what we needed and he assured me his company could handle the job!

Within 90 days we had our new program up and running and began marketing it to the mortgage community!

THANK YOU, LORD!

I HAVE A PAST LIFE REGRESSION

One evening I watched with fascination as a weekly prime-time program devoted the entire hour to the issue of reincarnation. I couldn't believe it! A prime-time show on reincarnation? Maybe people were beginning to open their minds a little!

The issue related to people who suffered from various phobias or pains that resisted any medical treatment. Several clinical psychologists explained that when these people were regressed and taken to a previous lifetime where they suffered a traumatic death, once they relived the traumatic incident their pains, illnesses and phobias disappeared.

One psychologist told the story of a woman who constantly felt like she was choking to death, despite the fact that all medical tests could find nothing wrong with her. She experienced a past life in which she was strangled to death and after reliving that experience the feeling of choking just disappeared! The results were amazing! Many of these patients experienced total recovery after going through a past-life regression!

I began wondering about the sharp pain in the upper right side of my back that had been plaguing me since I was rear-ended in an automobile accident back in 1985. The pain had resisted any and all medical treatments. I wondered if the pain could be caused by something that happened to me in a former lifetime, so I contacted Jack Moon, the gentleman who helped me so many years previously, and scheduled an appointment for a past-life regression.

I don't know what I expected, but I was totally unprepared for what transpired!

In my first past-life regression I saw myself as a male dressed like a slave in the time of the Roman Empire and I was desperately running, trying to escape capture. I was eventually captured and thrown into a dungeon and I could smell the dampness and the scent of straw as I lay there.

Eventually I was dragged out of the dungeon by Roman soldiers and taken to an arena, where my hands and feet were tied between two posts. A Roman soldier demanded that I renounce my belief in Christ or suffer death.

The Roman soldier was my ex-husband! I couldn't believe it! I refused to renounce my belief in Christ despite all of the torture inflicted upon me by this soldier. When he realized that I wasn't going to do what he wanted me to do, he took his spear and threw it at me.

The spear pierced my upper right chest and came out my back — ***exactly at the spot where I still suffer pain to this day!*** And still I remained standing despite the spear through my chest.

The Roman soldier (my ex-husband) was infuriated when he saw that I would not fall down, so he came behind me, took his sword, and hit me behind my knees, forcing me to collapse. At that point I died.

I then relived a second lifetime in which I was a male during the time that knights and jousting were popular. I

It Is Done!

was a knight who was well respected by my peers and once again *my ex-husband was there as a knight as well!*

Apparently he was jealous of the respect I had among the other knights, and it also appeared that he and I were both pursuing the affections of the same woman.

Strangely enough, that woman was my ex-husband's second wife in our current lifetime. I had met her a few years previously and we really hit it off and kept in touch with each other. Now I understood why I liked her so much — I knew her in a former lifetime!

In that lifetime my ex-husband and I were in a jousting match together. I saw myself riding a horse with my jousting spear pointed toward my opponent, but he was faster and his spear pierced my chest and came out of my back, once again *at the very spot where I was currently experiencing pain!*

I fell off my horse and the woman we were both interested in rushed to my side and buried her head in my chest, crying. I looked at my ex-husband and saw such hatred and anger coming from him when he realized that this woman loved me. I then died.

I relived a third lifetime when I was once again a male during the time of the Old West. I was sitting alone at a campfire one evening when I was captured by a group of Indians and taken to their camp. The chief of that tribe was — oh no! — my ex-husband! He tied me to a post and personally took a spear and — yep, you guessed it — threw it at my chest, where it exited through my back *at*

exactly the same spot I had been hit by him twice before! I died wondering why the chief was so angry with me and feeling that I had done nothing to deserve this horrible death.

When I came out of my regressions I was shocked that I had experienced three lifetimes, all as a male, all with my ex-husband, in which he had ended up killing me! Now here I was in a fourth lifetime where he didn't kill me physically but he had tried to destroy me financially. What was this all about?

I remembered the vision I had many years earlier where I was sitting in a garden with Jesus and he asked me to forgive my ex-husband, telling me that he would take care of the $50,000 debt. (That debt was eventually settled for $10,000, which was better than $50,000! I was grateful that I had the money to pay it!)

Was this about forgiveness? I had come to believe that we live many lifetimes in which we learn lessons and will have to repeat those lessons through many more lifetimes until we learn them. In all of these lifetimes had I been unable to forgive him?

My past-life regression gave me much food for thought and I began making a concerted effort to forgive my ex-husband. Several years have passed since then and I'm still suffering the pain in my back.

Recently in our Wednesday night Prayer Circle I asked once again for guidance. I was told that it was not just an issue of forgiveness, but an issue of ***LOVE.***

It Is Done!

I must learn to love him as well as forgive him. I'm still working on that issue and trust that I'll resolve it in this lifetime. I would hate to think that I must come back in yet another lifetime with him and repeat some horrible experience before I learn this lesson!

THE MIRACLES CONTINUE

I have watched with great joy and pleasure as my staff has responded to God's wonderful gifts and blessings with such an open willingness to accept. It makes things so much easier when everybody jumps to "affirm" any and everything!

After the September 11 tragedy my business slowed down, as I'm sure everyone's did. In October I was scheduled to fly to Raleigh to do a class in-house for a mortgage company. On that Wednesday as I was running out the door to catch a plane, I stopped at the Receptionist's desk to check on the number of students who were signed up for the class that began the following Monday.

I was shocked and dismayed to see that there were only 20 students in a class that normally numbered at least 50! Oh, my gosh! That class was an important "anchor" class that helped pay my monthly overhead! Twenty people just wasn't acceptable!

I looked at my two employees in the Receptionist area and said, *"Twenty people for that class is totally unacceptable! We'll do an affirmation right now! 'Lord, we affirm that class is totally and completely filled up. We thank You for bringing the students to us and we thank You for the opportunity to convey valuable information to these students. Thank You, Lord!* ***IT IS DONE!****'"*

My two staff members also repeated ***"IT IS DONE!"*** and I ran out the door to catch my plane. I didn't give it much thought until Thursday afternoon after my training

It Is Done!

session when I called the office to see how everything was going.

My Receptionist said, *"Gee! Did we have to affirm so strongly? These phones have been ringing off the hook! We signed up **27 MORE PEOPLE** for Monday's class and the calls are still pouring in! We're all frantically trying to get everyone registered!"*

On Wednesday we had 20 people signed up for that class. By Friday we had **56 PEOPLE! THANK YOU, LORD!**

I now have a staff of customer service representatives who contact mortgage companies nationwide to market my books, videos and classes, and they all do a terrific job. My Sales Manager tells me that anytime things get slow and they're not getting enough business they all gather together to do their **"*affirmations.*"**

As a group they all thank God for the business that is pouring in and thank Him for the opportunity to help these people who need our products and services. Every time they perform this ritual, **THE PHONES IMMEDIATELY BEGIN RINGING OFF THE HOOK!**

The greatest joy of my life has been the opportunity to share my miracles with the members of my staff and help them understand that the miracles that God provides for me are available to them also, if they will just ask.

I began gathering my staff together for a monthly Goal Setter Meeting, encouraging them to state certain desires or goals they would like to see occur within the next month. I write down these goals and desires for each person and we all verbally repeat that person's goals, affirm them, and say *"IT IS DONE!"*

The most difficult part is convincing them that they **DESERVE** whatever they desire, as long as it doesn't hurt them or anyone else. Most of the women have children, and the tough part is getting them to ask for something for **THEMSELVES**, rather than for one of their children.

In trying to convince them that it is not selfish to ask for something for themselves, I use the analogy of airline flight attendants always instructing the passengers that, in the event of a problem that requires the use of the oxygen mask, *they are to put the mask on themselves first before helping their children.* The happier we are with ourselves, the more we help ourselves first, the more we will be able to share this happiness and good fortune with others.

One of my employees is a young divorced mother with a small baby. Jessie had been living with her parents trying to save a little money and in one of our Goal Setter meetings she expressed a desire to find an apartment that she could afford. We all affirmed the perfect apartment for her that was close to the office and would not cost more than $650 per month.

The Monday following our Goal Setter meeting, Jessie came running into my office and started telling me about the apartment she had found that weekend.

She said, *"I was driving down the road on my way to the store when I felt a strange urge to pull into the apartment complex that I've driven past a million times. It was such a beautiful complex with a security gate, beautiful landscaping, clubhouse, pool...you know what I mean. I always figured the rent for those apartments would be way out of my price range but I just felt this strange urge to pull in.*

"When I went in and told the apartment manager what I was looking for, she told me she had just the apartment — and it was only $620 per month! I just can't believe it, Kathy! These affirmations really work!"

On another occasion I stopped my Office Manager, Debbie, in the hallway and asked how she was coming in her attempt to find her daughter a car. Debbie lamented that she wasn't having any luck finding a good car in the $3,000 price range.

I responded, *"Then we will affirm the perfect car right now! Lord, we thank You for the perfect car for Debbie's daughter. A car that is dependable, a car that is in good shape, and a car that Debbie pays no more than $3,000 for. Thank You, Lord!* ***IT IS DONE!"***

After completing our affirmation, one of our staff walked out of his office and said, *"I couldn't help but overhear you. I have a 1995 Honda that I was just about to put up for sale. It's a good little car and I was going to ask $3,000 for it. Debbie, are you interested?"*

I looked at Debbie and said, *"Was that fast enough for you?"*

Debbie said, *"I knew God worked fast. I just didn't know He worked that fast! Thank You, Lord!"*

And still the miracles continue! I was able to more than double my current office space while increasing my monthly rent only 50% above what I had been paying! ***Thank You, Lord!***

I was negotiating with my current landlord to expand my office space into the office to the left of my existing space, and because he offered me such a good deal I was also able to take the space on the right side as well!

That space has become my ***"Capstone Spiritual Foundation"*** and gives me the opportunity to offer many spiritual classes.

Several women who attend our Wednesday night Prayer Circle now have a private office to conduct their spiritual consultations and we are able to offer books and tapes on spiritual topics.

I am so grateful that God has been with me through my spiritual journey and I look forward to the opportunity to share the many wonderful miracles He has performed in my life. My greatest desire is to let everyone I come in contact with know that ***miracles can happen every day in their lives, just as they have in mine!***

THANK YOU, LORD! IT IS DONE!

It Is Done!

Kathy Lewis is the founder and president of Capstone Institute of Mortgage Finance. With more than 30 years of experience, Kathy has built Capstone into the nation's premier training institute for the mortgage banking and real estate industry.

Before founding Capstone, Kathy worked as a loan officer for a major lending institution, where she was consistently among the top producers. While working as an on-site sales agent for a national builder, she sold more than 160 homes within a 12-month period when interest rates were at 16%! She spent five years as vice president of one of Atlanta's largest homebuilders, and was president of a mortgage company before founding Capstone Institute in 1986.

A self-proclaimed "seeker of truth" for the past 25 years, Kathy credits much of her success to her knowledge and implementation of spiritual principles and values. With a desire and commitment to help others build successful careers and meaningful lives, she founded Capstone Spiritual Foundation in 2002. "My vision for the Foundation," says Lewis, "is to help people positively transform their lives through the understanding and practice of spiritual laws and principles."

Kathy is the author of more than 32 textbooks pertaining to all aspects of mortgage finance. *It Is Done! — Miracles Still Happen!* is her first book which chronicles her own inspiring journey of self-discovery. It provides many empowering ideas and insights to spiritual seekers at all levels.

In addition to her motivational speaking engagements, Kathy currently offers workshops which examine these spiritual principles more in-depth, and consulting services for those who want to create successful business enterprises "the enlightened way."